The ATHLETE'S GUIDE TO SPONSORSHIP

How to find an individual, team or event sponsor

BY JENNIFER E. DRURY, ATTORNEY AT LAW

co-authored by Cheri Elliott, Professional Cyclist

VELO
press

Boulder, Colorado USA

THE ATHLETE'S GUIDE TO SPONSORSHIP

Copyright © 1996, 1998 by Jennifer E. Drury

International Standard Book Number: 1-884737-78-1

Library of Congress Cataloging-in-Publication Data:

Drury, Jennifer E., 1970 –
    The athlete's guide to sponsorship: how to find an individual, team, or event sponsor / written by Jennifer E. Drury; with contributions by Cheri Elliot. — 2nd ed.
      p.   cm.
    Includes bibliographical references (p.) and index.
    ISBN 1-884737-78-1
    1. Sports sponsorship.   2. Sports – Marketing.   I. Elliot, Cheri, 1970 – .
II. Title.
    GV716.D78   1998
    796' .079'73–dc21   98–5582
                                               CIP

Printed in the USA

VELO
press

1830 N. 55th Street • Boulder, CO • 80301-2700
303/440-0601 • Fax 303/444-6788 • E-mail velopress@7dogs.com

To purchase additional copies of this book or other VeloPress titles, call 800/234-8456 or visit us on the web at www.velogear.com.

Cover photos by Robert Oliver

About the Authors

Jennifer Drury is an attorney in private practice at Drury Law Firm and president of JED Sports Management. Her firm represents and consults several top professional athletes in a variety of alternative and extreme sports. Additionally, Ms. Drury provides general legal services to corporations and commercial businesses, including domestic and international trademark, patent, and copyright services.

Ms. Drury obtained her J.D. from the University of the Pacific, McGeorge School of Law in Sacramento, California. Ms. Drury is an active member of the Sports Lawyer's Association, the National Sports Law Institute, the International Sports Summit, and the Women's Sports Foundation.

Cheri Elliott is both a nationally and internationally famed cyclist. Cheri carries with her an impressive collection of National and World titles including three NORBA National titles, two gold Medals at the ESPN Extreme Games, and a Bronze medal finish at the 1998 UCI Downhill World Championships. Additionally, she carries with her a Bicycle Motocross (BMX) history that has her forever branded as a "living legend." Currently, Cheri is paving another legendary path in the sport of mountain biking. Cheri is not only a top athlete, she also holds a bachelor's degree in Business, and graduated with honors from California State University in Sacramento.

Contents

(Chapter Nine cont.)

Acknowledgments

This book was an exciting project from cover to cover. There are several wonderful people who contributed their time and effort to make this book a success.

First, thank you to my parents, William and Lilian, and my siblings, Alison and Ricky, for always believing in me and encouraging me to follow my dreams. You are all the greatest. Also, thank you to Linda and Doug, the best in-laws anyone could ever have. The tranquillity of your garden provided a haven for me when I needed peace and quiet to work on this book.

A very special thank you to all the people who were interested in this project and took the time to discuss issues with me and provide me with usable quotations. The readers are lucky to learn from you all. A special thanks to Peggy Welch and Margo Carroll of M2 Images for their contribution of photos to the book. Special thanks to my good friend Susanna who provided moral and editorial support throughout the drafting of both the first and second editions.

Last of all, a *very* special thanks to Cheri both for your insightful contributions and personal dedication. Without you, this book would never have become a reality. Thank you.

Warning — Disclaimer

This book is designed to provide information in regard to the subject matter covered. The information provided should not be considered a substitute for legal or other professional services. If legal or other expert assistance is required, the services of a competent professional should be sought.

It is not the purpose of this manual to reprint all the information that is otherwise available to the author.

Every effort has been made to make this manual as complete and accurate as possible. However, there may be mistakes both typographical and in content.

The purpose of this manual is to educate. The author shall have neither liability nor responsibility to any person or entity with respect to any loss or damage caused, or alleged to be caused, directly or indirectly by information contained in this book.

FOREWORD

Are you an athlete who has never been sponsored? Or, are you an athlete who is already sponsored and looking to find an eye-wear sponsor or a shoe sponsor? Maybe you are tired of paying high prices for products that you feel you can get for free or at a discount. Whatever the case, whether you are a beginner or professional, young or old, male or female, already sponsored or never been sponsored, your chances for sponsorship are about to improve.

When evaluating your sponsorship potential it is important to understand that your opportunities depend not only on your talent as an athlete, but also on "who" and "what" you know. This book is going to give you the "what," which will inevitably lead you to the "who."

The following is an outline of the STEP-by-STEP process for getting sponsored. Think of it as a business plan. Each step that you successfully complete will bring you closer to your goal of getting sponsored.

STEP 1: Determine your objectives

STEP 2: Make a contact list and do the research

STEP 3: Establish budgets

STEP 4: Develop your proposal

STEP 5: Send the proposal(s)

STEP 6: Do necessary follow up(s)

STEP 7: Send thank you(s) and keep your sponsors informed

Each of these steps is equally important and extensively covered in chapter 2. The second chapter is by far the most important chapter because it will help get your foot in the door.

Chapters 3 through 6 will keep the door from slamming on

your foot. Chapter 3 is called "What Can You Do for the Sponsor?" It confirms that sponsorship is a give-and-take relationship. Chapter 4, "The Do's and Don'ts of Sponsorship," gives you tips on keeping and/or impressing your sponsors. Chapter 5, "Negotiating Your Deal," gives you simple tips and guidelines for negotiations. Chapter 6 is called "Contracts." This chapter offers tips on understanding contract formats and terms.

Chapter 7, "Alternatives to Sponsorship," is for those of you interested in competing for discounts on products or riding for local teams. Chapter 8, "Who Needs a Manager?" answers questions about personal management for athletes.

Chapter 9, "Marketing a Sports Team," is a comprehensive chapter that provides a STEP-by-STEP process for proposal writing and sponsorship planning. Chapter 10, "Marketing a Sporting Event," provides a simple overview of this area of marketing and is designed as an introduction to the topic, not a comprehensive guide.

Lastly, Chapter 11, "Dealing with the Media," introduces the reader to basic concepts and strategies for talking with the media. The principles outlined in this chapter are intended to assist the individual athlete, team manager, or event coordinator with his or her publicity strategy.

In addition, this book contains "Quick Tips." These are highlighted boxes that contain easy-to-read tips for easy reference.

For your convenience, appendices have been purposely added as "worksheet" pages. This will allow you to use *The Athlete's Guide to Sponsorship* as a workbook. Write down your ideas and thoughts as you read the book and use your own notes as references. *The best business ideas can be lost when not written down right away.* The special binding also allows easy note taking; it allows the reader to lay the book flat.

CHAPTER one

DEFINING SPONSORSHIP

Spon·sor (s... ...who takes the ...responsibil... ...other person or thing. 2. A ...godparent. 3. A business that... ...dio or ...television program in return for advertising time ...—sponsor ... sponsorship

Sponsorship is a broad term which generally means to provide *support* to *another.* In sports sponsorship the word "support" can mean a variety of things: discounts on products, product donations, performance and media bonuses (incentives), entry fee stipends, travel expenses, or salaries. In addition, the word "another" can be just about anyone or anything. Companies can provide support to amateur and/or professional athletes, teams, or events. All of these different types of sponsorships are considered part of sports marketing.

For decades, sporting goods companies have enhanced their marketing efforts through athlete endorsements and other sports promotion. In recent years, non-sport companies have entered sports marketing in an attempt to heighten consumer awareness of their products.

There are many reasons why companies sponsor athletes and sporting events. The main reason is to sell their products. By sponsoring a certain sport or event, companies hope to raise consumer awareness of a certain product or products.

Additionally, companies hope that consumer awareness will eventually lead to brand loyalty; that is, that people will buy a certain product because (1) they like the athletes who endorse it, or (2) they appreciate the company supporting the sport. Some companies sponsor athletes and events to create community good will. Again, however, the bottom line is profit for the company. If the company did not turn a profit as a result of sports sponsorship, it would have no budget for sports marketing efforts.

The phenomenon of brand loyalty is the main reason why athletes and sporting events obtain sponsorships. Something you should always remember is that once you are a sponsored athlete you are a spokesperson for the company and for its products. The company relies on *you* to make a good impression on the community so that the community's awareness of the company is positive.

As mentioned above, there are three main types of sports sponsorship: individual, team, and event. Each will be discussed briefly here and developed later in respective chapters. The main focus of this book, however, is athlete sponsorship.

INDIVIDUAL ATHLETE SPONSORSHIP

Many different sponsorship levels exist for athletes. Before you go any further, you need to figure out which level corresponds to your needs and capabilities and then tailor your sponsorship proposal around it. The Sponsorship Diagram in Table 1-1 displays the basic athlete sponsorship levels and categories of sponsorship.

CHERI ELLIOTT, PROFESSIONAL MOUNTAIN BIKE RACER

Mark Langton, 1997

Table 1-1 Sponsorship diagram

| | CATEGORY 1 | CATEGORY 2 | CATEGORY 3 | CATEGORY 4 | CATEGORY 5 |
	Discounts	Free Products	Expenses Paid	Bonuses and Contingencies	Salaries
LEVEL 1	X				
LEVEL 2	X	X			
LEVEL 3	X	X	X		
LEVEL 4	X	X	X	X	
LEVEL 5	X	X	X	X	X

The top row represents the different categories of sponsorship. The levels down the left column of the chart represent the different levels of athletes. Levels 1 and 2 typically represent beginners and amateurs. Levels 3 and 4 represent top experts and lower end professionals. Levels 1, 2, 3, 4, and 5 are typically representative of a combination of sponsorships that top professionals receive. This chart will be discussed in detail in subsequent chapters. Specifically, chapter 5, "Negotiating Your Deal," discusses categories 1 to 5 in detail.

TEAM SPONSORSHIP

Team sponsorship is a little bit different from athlete sponsorship. With team sponsorship, a group of people is sponsored and represents a brand or a company together; whereas with athlete sponsorship, athletes are sponsored individually. Companies find team sponsorships desirable because the impact of exposure can be greater. However, team sponsorships usually cost more for the sponsor because there are more people involved and the team's needs are greater than those of an individual athlete.

As with athlete sponsorships, there are different levels in team sponsorship. These levels are discussed in detail in Chapter 5.

Margo Carroll, M2 Images

TEAM SPONSORSHIP IS AN OPTION IN A VARIETY OF SPORTS.

EVENT SPONSORSHIP

Event sponsorship is significantly different from athlete and team sponsorship, but the same basic principles apply. The sponsorship of sports events provides an additional opportunity for companies to create public awareness of their products and to create community good will.

Event coordinators are the people who seek out sponsorship for events, not athletes or team managers. Event coordinators, however, often hire sports marketing firms to prepare sponsorship proposals, target potential sponsors, and negotiate deals. The main reason that event coordinators seek sponsorship is to help pay for production of the event.

Potential sponsors usually have the opportunity to sponsor the entire event or only a portion of the event. For example, if the National Off-Road Bicycle Association (NORBA) offered sponsorship to a company, it may offer sponsorship of the entire National Championship Series or sponsorship of just the cross-country portion of the series. The potential sponsor could choose the scope of its sponsorship according to its target market and budget.

Event sponsorship is just as important as individual athlete and team sponsorship. For without events, there would be no opportunities for athletic competition.

Margo Carroll, M2 Images

MAXXIS TIRES WAS AN EVENT SPONSOR OF THIS DOWNHILL MOUNTAIN BIKING EVENT IN PARK CITY, UTAH.

CHAPTER two

THE STEP-BY-STEP
PROCESS

Following is an outline of the STEP-by-STEP process for getting sponsored. Think of it as a business plan. Each step that you successfully complete will bring you closer to your goal. Follow each step every time you approach a sponsor for sponsorship. Creating a quality proposal is time consuming but the more thorough your research and detailed your proposal, the better your chances of success. Having a good grasp on the whole process also will aid you in creating and executing a sponsorship plan that will work for you.

STEP 1: Determine your objectives

STEP 2: Make a contact list and do the research

STEP 3: Establish budgets

STEP 4: Develop your proposal

STEP 5: Send the proposal(s)

STEP 6: Do necessary follow up(s)

STEP 7: Send a thank you(s) and keep sponsors informed

STEP 1:

DETERMINE YOUR OBJECTIVES

Answering the question, "What are my objectives?," begins the sponsorship process. To help you determine your objectives and goals, answer the following questions and analyze your response to each:

• *Am I an amateur or a professional?*

Labeling yourself as an amateur or a professional will immediately narrow down the types of sponsorships available to you. The chart in the introduction lists five levels of athletes; use that chart to determine the types of sponsorship available for an athlete of your caliber.

• *How long have I been active in my sport?*

If you are a beginner, you do not have as much bargaining power as a seasoned athlete. Alternatively, if you have been competing for a few years you will most likely find that you have more leverage than the beginner. Sponsors like fresh faces, but they also enjoy working with athletes who already know the ropes.

• *What are my best results?*

The resume worksheet in Appendix B will assist you in organizing your competition history. Just like applying for any job, you will have to provide the potential sponsor a resume which outlines your qualifications. Your past results and your level of competition will help you determine what you can ask of a sponsor in your proposal.

• *Will I be competing fulltime or only at some events?*

This question should be easy to answer. Do you plan to compete only in the state in which you live? Or will you compete in your region, the nation, or the entire world? Your proposal will include a competition schedule, so you will have to decide what your plans are for the year. Drafting a competition schedule is discussed in detail in this chapter under Step 4.

• What can I offer a company in return for sponsorship?

You will have to brainstorm about the different things that you can offer a sponsor in return for sponsorship. This subject is discussed in detail in chapter 2. Remember, if you are not a top professional you will have to offer more than a guaranteed winner or the right to use your name and likeness in their advertising campaign.

• Do I need money to support my competition? How much?

Mark Langton, 1997

Determining your competition budget is Step 3 of the STEP-by-STEP process and is discussed in detail later. Keep in mind, however, that a budget is necessary. Having a budget planned before you begin your search will give you a great starting point for developing the terms of your proposal.

CHERI ELLIOTT IS ONE OF THE MOST HEAVILY SPONSORED ATHLETES IN MOUNTAIN BIKING.

• Do I need any specific products to support my competition? What kinds of products?

Before you start contacting potential sponsors, make a list of all the different products you will need to compete: equipment, energy bars, clothing, nutritional supplements, etc. Having a comprehensive list of all the products you need will help you target potential sponsors.

Peggy Welch, M2 Images

DETERMINE WHAT EQUIPMENT YOU WILL NEED TO COMPETE. FOR EXAMPLE, PROFESSIONAL MIKKI DOUGLASS NEEDS A BIKE, HELMET, GOGGLES, MISCELLANEOUS COMPONENTRY AND A CERTAIN TYPE OF CLOTHING.

• *Do I have any sponsorship connections already?*

If you already have sponsorship connections, you should start your search by contacting them first. By contacting those whom you already know and have good relationships with, you start your search on the firmest ground possible.

• *Am I looking for team or individual sponsorship?*

Your decision to seek out team or individual sponsorship

may be determined by the fact that in your sport there are *only* teams or *only* individual athletes. If the sport in which you compete has both team opportunities and individual opportunities, then you have a decision to make. Will you seek out only team sponsorships? Or, will you look for individual sponsors (i.e. a different sponsor for each product or equipment component)? If you are trying to obtain a team sponsorship, your search for individual, smaller sponsorships should be postponed until after you obtain team support. This is because teams are often funded by co-sponsors and team athletes are bound to represent the team's co-sponsors.

It is important to remember that not all sponsors follow the five-tier system outlined in Table 1-1. Some only have two tiers: salaried professionals and pro-deals (discounts to athletes on equipment and other competition necessities). You want to avoid overreaching whenever possible. As will be discussed later, you must be familiar with the companies to which you are writing and be sensitive to their established budgets and programs.

Decide what your goals are before you go any further. BE SURE TO FAIRLY EVALUATE YOUR WORTH AS AN ATHLETE AND DO NOT ASK FOR TOO MUCH. THIS COULD TURN OFF PROSPECTIVE SPONSORS.

STEP 2

MAKE A CONTACT LIST AND DO THE RESEARCH

Once you have an understanding of your objectives, you need to begin the research phase of the STEP-by-STEP process. Begin by making a list of the companies and products that you are interested in endorsing and doing some simple research.

Get all the relative information from the potential sponsor that you need to draft a professional, personal proposal. You will use the information that you obtain to draft your cover letters, send the proposals, and make the necessary follow-ups.

MAKE A CONTACT LIST

Make a list of all the products and companies you are interested in endorsing. Start by jotting down the names of the products and companies that you like most. Next, look through magazines, visit local sports shops, go to vendor booths at sports events and attend industry trade shows to get ideas. By going beyond the boundaries of your current knowledge, you may come across certain products and companies that you may not have thought of by making a list from memory alone. Have fun with this part of the process. Remember, no list is too big or too small!

FIND THE PHONE NUMBERS AND ADDRESSES

Once you have made your contact list, find the telephone numbers and addresses of each company; you often will be able to find a toll-free number. You most likely will be making several calls, so the more money you can save with toll-free numbers, the better. These numbers can usually be found in magazine advertisements, sports directories, toll-free information (1-800-555-1212) or even on a web site. Be aware, however, that some companies intend their toll-free numbers be used only for sales calls. If the receptionist tells you that this is the case and that you must call the direct number, you should. When you call, be sure that you obtain the correct mailing address of each company so that you can ensure your proposals arrive safely.

One way to get information about companies is to look each

of them up on the Internet. Not all businesses have web sites, but if you have access to the Internet you should try this approach first. You can find out a lot of valuable information on a web site. Also, you can often send e-mail to a company, ask questions and receive a timely response. This approach will save you both time and money.

CALL EACH COMPANY

You should call each company and say to the first person who answers the phone, "Hi. Can you please tell me who to contact regarding sports sponsorship?" Make sure you ask for the proper spelling of the contact person's name. You will appear careless and ill-informed if you send a proposal to someone and misspell his or her name. Also, be sure of whether you are sending your proposal to a man or a woman and use the correct prefix (i.e., Mr. or Ms.). Next, ask for the address if you do not have it or confirm the address that you do have. This initial phone call should last no longer than two or three minutes. Make it as short and simple as possible. Do not attempt to talk to the sponsorship contact at this time, and do not identify yourself. The medium-sized company gets an average of 50 calls a day from people seeking sponsorship during the off season. If the receptionist puts you through to the contact, briefly state your interest in the company and let him or her know that you will be sending in a proposal. This will not happen very often, but when it does be sure to make a good impression by being brief and efficient.

WHAT IT MEANS TO MAKE A GOOD IMPRESSION

Making a good impression is imperative when asking someone to invest resources in you as an athlete. When communicating with a potential sponsor in any form (letter, e-mail, phone) try to come across as both intelligent and sincere. Have a game plan before you call. Know what you are going to say and what your intentions are before you take the first step to make contact. Remember that first impressions last! The companies have heard all the traditional "come on's" — avoid using them!

Here are some things that you can do to ensure that you make a good impression when communicating with a contact person:

• Create an outline of what you want to say ahead of time and have it in front of you when you call.

• Present yourself in an organized manner.

• Sound enthusiastic. People like to talk to others who are really excited about what they are saying.

• Be positive.

• Take good notes of the material you and the contact person discuss. This will help you later when you make follow-up calls or write your cover letter.

Occasionally the receptionist or sponsorship coordinator will ask you to fax your resume to them right away. If your resume and cover letter are complete, and you have access to a fax machine, go ahead and fax it. If your materials are incomplete or you do not have a fax machine, let them know that you would prefer to mail it to them. Always mail an identical copy of what you fax to the company. Faxes often get lost, and the copy subsequently received by mail will emphasize your interest in obtaining sponsorship.

Gather Other Research Information

When you contact a company regarding sponsorship it is a good idea to know something about the company, its policies, philosophies, and products. As one sponsorship coordinator commented, "It's not enough that the athlete call me and ask where to send his or her resume. When I read proposals I look for signs of product knowledge and/or product usage." If you are contacting a company for a snow board sponsorship, for example, you should be familiar with the company's different models of snow boards and state which one(s) you are interested in using for competition.

STEP 3

Establish a Budget for the Proposal Process and for Competition

Budgeting for the Proposal Process

Before you go any further, it will be helpful to set a budget for yourself. Determine how much money you can spend to get sponsored. Considerations should include postage, paper products, and phone calls. Use the list below to determine what you will need. Use the proposal budget worksheet in Appendix A to determine how much you can afford.

Items you will need to purchase:
- Resume paper
- Presentation folders (optional)
- Envelopes
- Number 10 envelopes (that match your resume paper)
- 9 x 12 envelopes (optional)
- Printing
- Photo reproduction (optional)
- Color copies, black and white copies, photo reproductions
- Video reproduction (optional)
- Postage

BUDGETING FOR COMPETITION

Budgeting for competition is one of the most important aspects of preparing your proposal. Unless you sign on with a team or group that is going to handle all of your travel and competition arrangements for you, you will be making your own plans. Establishing a target budget will help focus your proposal on reaching your goals and needs. By creating a budget you will be forced to figure out exactly how much money you need to compete. This will help you in the long run by ensuring that you will not have any surprises while on the road. Also, it will encourage you to book hotel rooms, rental cars, and airfare early so that you can benefit from less expensive prices.

You should create two budgets: a "what you actually need" budget and a "what you would want in an ideal world" budget. Basically, in your first budget you will have to determine how much money and equipment you will need at a minimum to compete. The second "in an ideal world" budget should consist of everything that you need and everything that you want to compete. Use the competition budget worksheets in Appendix A to draft each of these budgets. Also in Appendix A is an event budget worksheet. You should make several photocopies of this page and fill one out for each event you plan to attend during the year. Then, from these forms you will compile the information for the budget worksheet that covers the whole year of competition.

Some items to consider when figuring your competition budget are:
- Entry fees
- Travel expenses
- Airfare
- Highway tolls
- Hotel accommodations

- Food allowance
- Rental car
- Gasoline
- Competition and training equipment
- Competition clothing (uniforms)
- Masseuse/chiropractor
- Trainer/fitness consultant
- Gym membership
- Nutritional supplements/vitamins

TIPS FOR CUTTING CORNERS ON THE ROAD

If you are a dedicated amateur (or even neo-pro), you will probably do almost anything to get to your events. There are many ways in which you can save money while traveling. Most often, athletes combine resources with other athletes to save money. For example, instead of driving across country by yourself, find someone who is going to the same event and drive together. You can share rental cars, hotel rooms, gas money, and even food expenses.

Another way to save on expenses is to camp rather than rent a room at a hotel. Finding a site near the event location will not always be possible, but if you can find a camp site, this is a struggling athlete favorite money-saving tactic.

Professional mountain bike racer "Jammin'" Jennifer Zuener has some tips for saving money while on the road:

1. *Couch surfing — staying with friends while on the road*
2. *Camping — less expensive than staying at even the cheapest motels.*
3. *Shower at campgrounds. Most have 25¢ showers. If that fails, pools and hot tubs work well.*
4. *Eat pasta and bagels. They're cheap and quick to make.*

Peggy Welch, M2 Images

PROFFESSIONAL ATHLETE JENNIFER ZEUNER SPENT A FEW YEARS CAMPING AND COMPETING BEFORE SHE SIGNED A DEAL WITH A PRO-FESSIONAL TEAM.

5. *Keep a big cooler with fruit, snacks, etc. Be creative.*
6. *Lodging at the venue: Parking lots, pick-up truck beds.*
7. *VIP room — always a good place for good snacks.*

Lastly, plan your trips carefully. Even if you get a hefty travel budget from your sponsors, you will want to use that money wisely. Find the cheapest airfares (Three weeks advanced reservation is best), get economy rental cars, and do not order room service too often. Being frugal on the road will leave a little extra cash in your pocket in case a surprise event pops up that you really want to attend.

Now that you have your contact list, information on each company, and your budgets set, it is time to move on to the most important step — developing your proposal.

STEP 4

DEVELOPING YOUR SPONSORSHIP PROPOSAL

Developing your proposal is the most time-consuming part of the project. Do not rush yourself to get it done. A good presentation will take time and patience.

The five key elements of an individual athlete sponsorship

Margo Carroll, M2 Images

JENNIFER ZEUNER, KATRINA MILLER AND SNOOPER CAMPING AT THE RACES.

proposal are:
- Cover letter
- Resume
- Venue-competition schedule
- Supplementary materials (photos, magazine articles, video, etc.)
- Additional materials for top professionals

This section discusses each of these elements in detail and provides samples from which you can create your own sponsorship proposal. It is important that your resume, cover letter, and supplementary materials express your individual talent and personality. In other words, be creative in conveying your image.

DEVELOPING YOUR RESUME

Begin the resume writing process by filling out the resume worksheet in Appendix B. You may want to make a copy of the worksheet so you can use it again next year. The worksheet has been designed to obtain information that will be transferred to the final draft of your resume. Upon subsequent review, this information also will help you determine your strongest skills and your most noteworthy achievements. Your completed resume should include most of the information from the worksheet. It is important to remember that you are asking a company to invest a portion of its sponsorship resources in you. This is your opportunity to sell yourself.

Next, combine all of your essential personal information into a format that you are comfortable with. Refer to the samples in Appendix C to develop a resume you are comfortable with and that will stand out above the rest.

1. Heading/Personal Information

Your resume will include some personal information at the

top of the page, including your name, complete address, phone and fax numbers, and e-mail address. Other types of personal information such as height, weight, or age should not be included.

The resume worksheet in Appendix B contains a space for you to put any nicknames that you have. If you have a nickname, you will have to decide whether or not you want to use it in your proposal

MISSY "THE MISSILE" GIOVE.

materials. Some nicknames are appropriate and should be used, while others should be avoided at this preliminary stage. First, you only want to use nicknames that are relevant to who you are as a person. For example, a professional mountain bike racer goes by the name of Missy "the Missile" Giove. Her real name is Melissa Giove. She adopted this nickname from the fact that she is a very fast and spirited racer. The Missile is a great example of someone who should include her nickname in the proposals that she sends because it underscores her image.

2. Competition Results

Your resume should chronologically list your competition results. You will begin with the most recent and work your way backward a year or two. In this section you will want to list the competition's name, the date and location of the event, the category that you competed in, and your individual placing. The best way to list your results is to create a graph or grid and insert the information. This will make your resume easy to read. The sample resumes in Appendix C illustrate this concept.

Listing your competition history in your resume is very important. Potential sponsors want to know what you have done in the past so that they can gauge your future potential. However, do not let this part of the proposal writing process discourage you. If your competition history is limited, or if your results are not terrific, you simply will have different sponsorship expectations than a successful professional. For example, with limited competition history and average results you should categorize yourself in Level One or Level Two of the Sponsorship Diagram (Table 1-1). The cover letter that you draft will state the type of sponsorship that you are seeking and your resume will confirm whether or not your credentials merit such support.

3. Achievements and Awards

Just as potential sponsors are interested in knowing your competition history, they are equally interested in knowing what awards or titles you have received within your sport and in other areas of your life. List your achievements either chronologically (starting with the most recent) or in order of significance. Again, refer to the sample resumes in Appendix B to see how these achievements are listed.

If you have earned a title in your sport (i.e. National Champion, Rookie of the Year, Most Improved) you may choose to highlight it at the top of the page beneath your name. Since most resumes will only receive a quick glance, you should highlight any qualities, achievements, or titles that will make you stand out from the rest of the applicants.

4. Special Additions and Abilities

Companies are also interested in the activities that you par-

Peggy Welch, M2 Images

LPGA GOLF PRO, LISA HORST, SHOWS OFF HER TALENT AS A CLIMBER.

ticipate in outside of competition. If you have abilities in some particular area other than your sport, listing them may provide the sponsor with (1) insight into you as an individual, and (2) new and creative marketing ideas. Companies are always interested in cross-marketing opportunities, so if you have some situation that fosters a cross-marketing opportunity then you should present that in your proposal. For example, if you own a local sports shop or run the local kids rodeo, then you may be able to develop a way to integrate your sponsorship into your shop or the rodeo. This provides the sponsor with additional marketing outlets and that is the main goal of sports sponsorship.

5. Education

List your most recent or current education first. Include the name(s) of the degree(s) that you received and the institution(s) from which you received it (them). If you earned a degree from a college, university, or vocational school, your high school information is not required.

Sponsors like to know your level of education for various reasons. If you do not have a degree, or if you did not graduate from high school, do not be alarmed. Education level is usually *not* a determining factor. However, if you possess a college degree or any other educational degree, it can be helpful to a potential sponsor. For example, sponsors can use the fact that you are a college graduate or a professional (doctor, lawyer, professor, CEO) to fashion an innovative advertising campaign. It's easy to imagine. There is a business person all decked out in business attire and a briefcase one day, and the next day he or she is off competing in an adventure race using XYZ company's climbing gear. That could be an effective advertisement for a company whose target market is the recreational athlete. Or, if you are still in high school a sponsor may be able to create an ad that shows you can be a student and an athlete simultaneously. The possibilities for advertising are endless. If you can present the potential sponsor with a unique marketing angle, you may find yourself a sponsored athlete.

6. References

You will want to prepare a list of at least three references. A reference is someone who can tell the sponsor about your talent, personal qualities, and work habits. A reference should be over the age of 18 and someone you have known for more than one year. If you do not have space, listing the references on your resume is not necessary. You may use the phrase "references available on request" as shown in the resume examples in Appendix C. If you have extra space on the resume once you have included all the required information, you can put the references directly on your resume. You should ask the reference beforehand if he or she is willing to be a reference for you. The resume worksheet in Appendix B will assist you in gathering all the necessary information.

When listing information under any of the resume categories, use brief, concise phrases. For the "experience" section, begin with an action word (a.k.a. verb). Avoid turning your resume into an autobiography. Refer to the sample resumes (Appendix C) for an example. Also, to save space on your resume avoid using the pronouns "I" and "me" in the text of your resume. Table 2-1 illustrates the use of action words and the absence of personal pronouns.

Table 2-1: Action Verb Usage Instead of Personal Pronouns

INSTEAD OF	USE
I had responsibility for the development of a new sport program.	Developed a new sport program.
My top finishes include second place in the Summer Extreme Games.	Finished second place in the Summer Extreme Games.
I was the National Champion in the expert class.	Attained the National Champion title in the expert class.
My accomplishments have exceeded my goals with podium finishes at every event.	Earned a podium position at every event, surpassing season goals.

It is very important that you avoid embellishing the truth on your resume. Never exaggerate your accomplishments. Lying on your resume will eventually come back to haunt you. If a company agrees to sponsor you in reliance on a misrepresentation that you made on your resume, your career as an athlete could be severely damaged by the bad publicity that will surface if the untruth is unveiled. Although you or others may think that little white lies are tolerable on a resume, they are not. You will not score points with a potential sponsor who either researches the accuracy of your representation or challenges it. You will only lose credibility — something that the business of sports sponsorship is built upon.

When drafting the text of your resume, keep the tone upbeat and positive. Sponsors like to work with athletes who have positive attitudes. Your resume is an opportunity to show them how terrific you are.

Lastly, type your resume in an appropriate format. Never send a handwritten resume. A handwritten resume is your way of saying "I don't care about getting a sponsor." The resume samples and sample resume headings in Appendix C provide a couple of format options. You will most likely print out several versions before coming up with the final copy, so do not waste your expensive paper printing out rough drafts. If you do not have access to a computer or word processor, check with the local college or copy store and try to rent one for a few hours. Professional resume services also are available for a fee.

Limit your resume to one page. Sponsors get many resumes each year and are inundated with paper. The recipient of your proposal will certainly appreciate brevity. Only if absolutely necessary should your resume extend to two pages, but it should never be more than two pages.

Once you finish typing the resume, run the document through a spell check program and ask a friend to read it over. Do anything possible to avoid presenting a resume with typographical or grammatical errors.

Be sure that your resume is appealing to the eye. You want the company to be impressed with you before they even read one word. First impressions make all the difference. Ask a few friends to look over your resume and tell you what their impressions are of the presentation.

Next, you have to purchase resume paper and envelopes. If your budget cannot afford this expense, print your resumes on nice, heavy white paper and use white envelopes. It is very important that your entire proposal looks professional and polished. If you can spend extra money to stand out and impress the company, consider purchasing 9x12 envelopes and presentation folders so you do not have to fold your presentation. Buying the larger envelopes is especially important if you are including photographs in your proposal.

Once you have developed your resume, a cover letter should be drafted to introduce you and the resume.

QUICK TIPS

- Be concise.
- Never send a hand-written resume.
- Show the potential sponsor your history.

DRAFTING YOUR COVER LETTER

The cover letter is one of the most important documents in the proposal. The main purpose of a cover letter is to introduce your entire presentation, establish that it is a proposal for sponsorship, introduce yourself and your attributes, and let them know why they should sponsor you. A good cover letter will grab the attention of the reader right away. Highlights and achievements should be stated briefly. Never write a cover letter that is more than one page. Companies get hundreds of requests for sponsorship —keep yours short and simple!

The main elements of a cover letter are:

Introductory paragraph

In this paragraph you will identify yourself and your interest in the company's product or service. You also will clearly state your interest in sponsorship.

First body paragraph

In this paragraph you will indicate how your background (experience), skills/abilities, education and persona enable you to be a quality spokesperson for the company.

Second body paragraph

In this paragraph you will describe your interest in the product or service and state what you want from the company. Do not beat around the bush. You should clearly state what you can offer the company in return for sponsorship (see chapter 3 for some ideas of what athletes can offer sponsors).

Concluding paragraph

In this paragraph, briefly state the materials which you have included in the proposal. You may then restate your interest in working with the company in the future. In your last sentence, indicate that you are hoping for a timely response. Also, use an active closing statement. Let them know that you will be following up within the next couple of weeks. Then, make sure that you do follow-up!

COVER LETTER CHECK LIST

• *Write to someone in particular*

Never send a cover letter "To Whom it May Concern" or use some other impersonal opening. If you do this, your letter will probably be treated like junk mail and tossed in the trash. To avoid this, do the research recommended in Step Two of the STEP-by-STEP process.

- *Make absolutely no errors*

One way to offend people quickly is to misspell their names or use an incorrect title. If there is any doubt, call and verify the correct spelling of names and other details before you send the letter. Also, review your letters carefully to be sure that they do not contain any typographical, grammatical, or other errors.

- *Personalize your content*

Most companies are not impressed by form letters of any kind, and you should avoid using them. Computer-generated form letters are often labeled as such and give the impression that you failed to do your research and/or that you are lazy. Companies do not want lazy people endorsing their products, so be sure to do your research and show knowledge of the company's product(s) in your cover letter.

- *Present a good appearance*

Your contact with potential sponsors should always be professional. Use quality stationery products. Use a printer or typewriter that prints clearly and does not smudge. Do not make your readers struggle to read the document — they will not do it, and your proposal will be put aside and probably rejected.

- *Use an appropriate format*

Always use a standard business correspondence format when drafting a cover letter. The letter examples in Appendices D and E show an appropriate style.

- *Have a friendly opening*

Begin your letter with a reminder of any prior contacts and state the reason for your present correspondence. If you have had no prior contacts, simply state the reason why you are writing.

- *Avoid the overuse of personal pronouns (I, me)*

Avoiding personal pronouns will not only shorten your resume, it will also allow you to emphasize sentences with action verbs.

- *Keep it simple*

Make your cover letter easy to read. Avoid the use of impressive words and long sentences. The easier you make it for the reader to read the letter, the more likely that he or she will read the entire document. Do not tell your life story in the cover letter, but simply mention the main points. Clearly express the purpose of your letter, your desires, and what you have to offer the company.

- *Define the next step*

When ending your letter, be sure to identify what you will do next. It is not always best to leave it up to the potential sponsors to contact you. Remember, they get hundreds of requests. Make it easy on them and let them know that you will follow-up. Close on a positive note and use a friendly closing.

Your presentation can be professionally complete with only a resume and a cover letter. However, if you are able to provide other materials to enhance your chances of getting sponsored, by all means include them in your proposal.

DRAFT A PROPOSED COMPETITION SCHEDULE

Including a list of the competitions and venues that you intend to attend will give the potential sponsor a better idea of how broad your exposure will be for them. The extent of your competitions and other appearances will have a lot to do with your rank as an athlete. It should also coincide with your sponsorship expectations. For example, if you are seeking sponsorship to compete in events located only in your state, then your exposure is limited quite a bit and that will reflect your overall value to potential sponsors. On the other hand, if you are a professional and plan to compete in the entire national circuit, then you are worth more to sponsors because your potential for exposure is greater. It should be pointed out that if you plan to compete on a local level, however, more local sponsors will be interested in you.

When compiling the list of events you plan to attend, limit the scope of the list to one year or season. Since most sponsorships last only one year (and are renewed annually), there is no reason to provide the sponsor with more information than needed. Your list should include any trade shows, conferences, or special events that you plan to attend during the year, as well. These sorts of events provide opportunities for sponsors to "show you off" and benefit from the marketing budget spent on you.

Often times you can obtain a competition schedule well in advance by contacting your sport's local, national, or international organizational body. A comprehensive venue-competition schedule will include the following: date of the event, name of the event, place of the event, and confirmed and expected media coverage of the event. Appendix F has a competition-venue schedule worksheet and Table 2-2 provides an illustration of a sample competition-venue schedule. You can adopt any format you want or copy the sample.

Table 2-2: Example of Venue-Competition Schedule

Date	Event	Place
May 15-16	National #1	Seattle, Washington
June 1-2	National #2	Mammoth Lakes, California
June 8-9	National #3	Pittsburgh, Pennsylvania
June 14	State Regionals	Fresno, California
July 10	National Finals	Phoenix, Arizona
August 12	State Finals	Big Bear Lake, California

Mark Langton, 1997

CHERI ELLIOTT SHOWS OFF HER UNIQUE ABILITY TO GET BIG AIR.

SUPPLEMENTARY MATERIALS THAT WILL ENHANCE YOUR PROPOSAL

Supplementary materials can enhance the overall presentation of your proposal. The exclusion of these items will not negatively affect your presentation or your chances of getting sponsored. On the other hand, the inclusion of any one of these items will give the company an opportunity to learn a little bit more about you, a potential spokesperson for its product or service. Whatever you do, do not overwhelm the potential sponsor by sending a bunch of paper. Send the minimum that will gain attention.

Supplementary Materials

Photographs (action or still)

Magazine or newspaper clips

Video (footage from a sports channel or really terrific home footage of your particular talents)

Demographics regarding the sport (i.e., TV coverage, number of spectators and average age of spectators). These demographics are not necessary when sending a proposal to a potential industry sponsor because they already know what is happening within the sport. Demographics are most useful

Margo Carroll, M2 Images

WHEELCHAIR RACER COMPETING IN DOWNHILL MOUNTAIN BIKE EVENT.

when contacting a company unrelated to your sport.

Any other unique items that represent you and your abilities (use your best judgment — do not include anything that is irrelevant or may be considered offensive).

Quick Tips

• Never send different-sized paper. Copy or color copy all photos and clippings on the same-sized paper as your resume and cover letter.

• Only use video if you have more than one showing on TV. Only use video if it is a significant clipping on a professional network and the focus is obviously on you. Do not just send one 10-second blurb. A company will be interested in consistency on TV, not just a once-in-a-blue-moon appearance.

Once you complete all the elements, the next steps are to put everything together and send the proposal off to a sponsor.

Step 5

Send The Proposal

Putting the Elements Together

Your cover letter, resume, and other materials should be put into the envelope in the following order:

1. Cover letter on top. Do not staple the cover letter to the resume.

2. Resume behind the cover letter. If the resume is more than one page, staple it.

3. All other materials should be placed beneath the cover letter and the resume.

4. Optional. Paper clip everything together. This may create less mess when the company representative opens the envelope. If you use a presentation folder, paper clipping is not necessary.

GETTING YOUR PROPOSALS OUT THE DOOR

Once your proposals have been assembled, place them in addressed envelopes. You have two options at this point:

1. Fold the proposal into thirds and put it in a regular number 10 envelope.

2. Spend a little extra money and put your proposal in a 9 x 12 envelope. If you really want to get fancy, consider purchasing presentation folders and placing the materials inside - this is definitely a way to make your proposal stand ou. Be aware, however, that presentation folders annoy some sponsorship contacts. If you are only sending a resume and a cover letter, you really have no reason to place the materials in a folder; it just makes more unnecessary work for the person receiving the proposal.

Before you send the proposal, record it on the proposal record sheet in Appendix G. You will also use the proposal record sheet to keep track of your follow-ups, conversations, and outcomes.

STEP 6

FOLLOW UP

After you have sent your proposal(s), wait approximately two to three weeks for a response. If you have not heard from the company, follow up with a phone call asking for the person to whom you directly sent the proposal. If you are unable to contact the correct person by phone, write a brief follow-up letter stating your continued interest in the company/product. Remind him or her of the proposal that you sent and of your interest in hearing back from them. (For a follow-up letter example, see Appendix G).

STEP 7

SEND A THANK YOU LETTER
AND KEEP YOUR SPONSORS INFORMED

Whether you were rejected right away, or signed a deal, always send a short thank you for the company's response and let them know that you will try again next year or that you are looking forward to working with them. This shows your respect for the company and improves your chances of being remembered when you submit proposals in the future. You should also send your sponsor(s) an occasional handwritten thank you when they send product on time or do something else that you really appreciate. (For examples of thank you letters, see Appendix E).

If you made a deal with a sponsor, one of the most important things to do during the term of the sponsorship is to keep them informed of your progress. Most sponsors really want to hear from the athletes that they provide money and/or product to and will value your updates. One of the best ways to keep sponsors informed is a newsletter. These updates do not have to be personalized to each sponsor, but they should be directed to your sponsors generally. A sample newsletter can be found in Appendix H. Sponsors frequently complain that the athletes they sponsor do not stay in touch after they receive their money or products. A great way to show your appreciation and respect for the company is to keep them informed (even if the news isn't so hot).

CHAPTER three

WHAT CAN YOU OFFER A SPONSOR?

Y ou must always remember that athlete sponsorship is a give-and-take relationship. It is not about what the sponsor can do for you, it is about what you can do for each other. More importantly, from the company's perspective, it is about how your sponsorship will result in product sales. If you always remember this, you will go far.

If you are someone that consistently competes and wins at the highest professional level, then you are offering the sponsor your talent and popularity. Unfortunately, there are only a handful of athletes in the world in each sport that can use this as their main selling point. And, sometimes the most talented athletes in the world do not obtain sponsorship because they cannot produce sales (i.e., a top professional may have such a poor public image that endorsements reflect badly on the company).

The following are some ideas of what you can offer a sponsor in return for sponsorship other than the normal use and endorsement of product. Of course, different sports have different needs, so be creative. These are only a few examples:

Mark Langton, 1997

THE JERSEY IN THIS PHOTO PROVIDES A GOOD EXAMPLE OF HOW TO
SELL LOGO SPACE ON COMPETITION CLOTHING. DIVIDE THE COMPE-
TITION CLOTHING INTO HYPOTHETICAL SEGMENTS AND SELL LOGOS BY
THEIR SIZE AND PLACEMENT.

JED Sports Management, 1996

SAMPLING PRODUCTS AT EVENTS OFFERS GREAT EXPOSURE TO YOUR
SPONSOR'S PRODUCT.

• Offer to place the sponsor's logo on your competition clothing.

• Work a few hours at the sponsor's booth at competition
venues, trade shows, and exhibitions.

• Work at the main office or factory part time.

• Offer at competition venues to give seminars or clinics that
highlight the sponsor's product(s).

• Convince the manager of the sports store that you work in
or shop at to carry the sponsor's products and assist in setting
up the deal.

• Be a mechanic for the team.

• Help manage the team when it's on the road.

• Help display product at event booths.

• Be a masseuse for the team.

• Allow the company to use your name and likeness in its
advertising campaign.

• Test and evaluate products.

• Offer help in research and development.

• Guarantee a win-ner.

• Guarantee loyalty and professionalism.

• Put your exceptional writing or speaking talent to work and help with ad copy or other promotional copy and appearances.

• Offer to sample the sponsor's product(s) at events - this a great idea for nutrition (food/drink) sponsors.

You should be able to come up with your own ideas about what you have to offer a sponsor. Consider your own special talents and background. For example, if you are a graphic artist by trade then you can offer the sponsor some design work in

Eric J. Horst, 1995

LPGA GOLF PRO LISA HORST.

exchange for sponsorship. As an athlete, you can offer potential exposure by putting on training camps for youths in your area. The possibilities are endless, and companies always appreciate fresh ideas. Be sure, however, to offer someting that will help with the company's bottom line (i.e., increase sales, improve image, cut down on miscellaneous expenses).

The most important thing is to offer the sponsor something that you can and will deliver. Nothing is worse than an empty promise. When you make a promise to your sponsor and you follow through, you build the rapport necessary for a positive, continuing relationship. When you fail to deliver what you promise, you lose credibility quickly and your chances for renewing your sponsorship diminish.

Work on building a relationship with your sponsor(s) that can last throughout your career in the sport. Pay close attention to the sponsorship tips in the next chapter. Some of the suggestions provided come to you directly from the top corporate sponsors in the world.

CHAPTER four

THE DO'S AND DON'TS
OF SPONSORSHIP

U sually, it's the little things that keep the sponsor relationship solid. Sponsors (at least most) do not expect
you to win every time you compete. What they do expect, however, is that you respect them, follow through on your promises, and promote their products to the best of your ability. If you
fail to respect the relationship with your sponsor, your deal
most likely will not be renewed the following year. To avoid this
from happening and to develop the necessary bond between
athlete and sponsor, you must always behave professionally
and be loyal to the companies and products that you endorse.
Use your common sense.

In compiling the data for this chapter, corporate sponsorship contacts from a variety of sports were asked to provide
two quotes, a sponsorship "do" and a sponsorship "don't." Their
comments are included at the end of each section. Read
through their quotes carefully because they contain valuable
information and then use this information in building quality
relationships with your sponsors.

SPONSORSHIP DO'S

- **KEEP YOUR SPONSOR INFORMED**

Let your sponsor know how you progress throughout the season. An up-to-date monthly newsletter really helps the sponsor with their own press releases to the media. Keeping in contact shows professionalism, enthusiasm, and respect and will most likely be a positive influence on their decisions for the following year. There is an example of a newsletter in Appendix H and a worksheet to assist you in drafting your own newsletter.

- **MAKE YOURSELF AVAILABLE**

Throughout the duration of your sponsorship, companies may need you for press conferences, photo shoots, team meetings, a body at the booth, clinics, or maybe even some dirty work. Be available when the sponsor needs your help. In fact, offer your help whenever possible. This is a good way to make a great impression and show your loyalty to the company.

- **ALWAYS BE PROFESSIONAL**

Remember that being a sponsored athlete is work, not play. It is a business and you are representing a company. Your professional conduct, respect for others, and ability to portray a positive image are the key ingredients. Even top athletes could never reach their sponsorship potential without behaving professionally. It is a fact that winning is not everything!

- **BE AHEAD OF SCHEDULE WHEN ORDERING PRODUCT**

Always let your sponsor know exactly what you need ahead of time. Companies are very busy and need your assistance in getting what you need on time. Polite follow-up phone calls or faxes are good reminders if you feel an order has not been sent. Most companies appreciate reminders when they are busy and will respond promptly. As always, however, do not be overbearing or annoying, this is a sure way to lose sponsorships fast.

- **FOLLOW THROUGH ON PROMISES**

You must produce what you have promised. Once you make a promise to a sponsor you have an obligation to follow through. If you fail to keep your promises, you will lose the respect of your sponsors.

- **SHOW YOUR LOYALTY TO EACH SPONSOR**

Loyalty is a key factor of the sponsorship relationship. Being loyal basically means not speaking negatively about the sponsor or its products. If you fail to show loyalty to your sponsors, you probably will not be resigning an agreement the following year.

- **KEEP TRACK OF EXPERIENCES WITH THE SPONSOR'S PRODUCTS**

Sponsors like to receive feedback from the athletes who endorse their products. Sometimes sponsored athletes are involved in testing new products. Keep a journal of aspects of the product(s) that you like and dislike. Also, if you have any suggestions for ways to improve the product(s), keep a record of that as well. Once a month, type up your comments and send them to your sponsor representatives. They are likely to appreciate and value your thoughts.

• **WEAR YOUR SPONSOR'S LOGO DURING COMPETITION AND TRAINING**

Make sure that the company feels as though it's getting its money's worth. Never wear a competitor's logo during competition or training.

• **SEND A THANK YOU**

When a sponsor does something special, send a thank you card. Let them know that you appreciate their efforts. You can also send a general thank you to all your sponsors in a newsletter.

SPONSORSHIP DO'S STRAIGHT FROM THE SPONSORS' MOUTHS

"Keep in touch with your manager, I like to hear from riders - not necessarily what place they finished, but also what they are up to. It is my job as a manager to relay what the team is doing back to the people who write the checks."
— ALAN FOSTER, BICYCLE TEAM MANAGER, AIRWALK FOOTWEAR.

"When reviewing sponsorship proposals, I like to see that the athlete has tried our product, they use it regularly, and can explain its benefits. This is a savvy athlete who will probably represent our interests well."
— CHRIS POLSTER, CNS INC. (BREATHE RIGHT)

"Send clippings, articles, and race results. Provide sponsors with recent photos that feature their products and make yourself available for photo-shoots and trade shows. This kind of attentiveness helps us determine the effectiveness of the sponsorship. The greater the exposure the athlete gets, the more like-

ly it is that he or she will receive sponsorship the following year."

— Taya Friedman, Senior Marketing Associate, Briko

"Nothing pleases a sponsor more than if their product is seen in a photo or on TV. Wear or hold the sponsored item when you are on the podium, during photo-shoots, and when you are giving interviews. Wear the product, always during competition, but also when you're engaging in leisure activities. The sponsor is sponsoring you in order to gain exposure for their product."

— Friedman, Briko

"When sending a sponsorship proposal to a potential sponsor, be sure to state what you can do for the sponsor in exchange for the sponsorship. Our objective is to sell more products, tell us how you can assist us in doing that."

— Tom Hillard, Sponsorship Director

"Researching a company before sending in a sponsorship proposal is very important. A lazy athlete is not someone we want representing our company. An athlete who calls me and asks where the resume should be sent, or about a product, has not spent much time researching the company. This information can be found anywhere, and these athletes are placed at the bottom of the pile."

— Chris Clinton, Sponsorhip Director,
Sachs Bicycle Components

SPONSORSHIP DON'TS

- **Don't use conflicting products**
  When you agree to be sponsored by a certain company with

certain products, do not conflict with this sponsorhip by using any similar products. This is not only offensive to the sponsor, it portrays an unfavorable image to potential future sponsors.

• Don't exhibit a negative attitude

If you are disappointed about something, if you are frustrated, if you lost a competition due to faulty equipment when you should not have, never show anger, disappointment, or unprofessional conduct in public. Remember that you are representing sponsors and that you are trying to impress potential sponsors. Do not blow your sponsorship by becoming known as someone with a bad attitude. Think before you act. Recall the main reason that companies sponsor athletes, to sell more products and gain public awareness. If the public views a sponsored athlete as a bad sport or poor role model, they may choose not to purchase products from that person's sponsors. This is referred to as brand disloyalty and is quite common.

• Don't speak negatively about the product

When you are a spokesperson for a product, it is your obligation to say positive things about the product publicly. Any problems a product may be having need to stay between the athlete and the company. Sometimes athletes test new products. If this is the case, you may experience some problems with the products you use. Keep notes on your experiences with new products and report any malfunctions to the company, not the public.

• Don't alter products

Respect the appearance and performance of all products given to you. Only when you and the sponsor mutually agree upon it, should any alterations occur. Never remove stickers or logos!

- ### Don't take advantage of your sponsors

Once you ink a sponsorship deal, stick to it. Do not attempt to change the terms of the sponsorship deal during the sponsorship. If you told the sponsor that you need five bikes, for example, do not go to them later in the year and ask for two more. Sponsors have a budget that they have to stick to in order for their program to work. If you change your needs mid-year, it will not be looked upon favorably. Never ask for more money during the season. You made a deal, live with it until the end of the year and be grateful for what you have.

- ### Avoid on-site solicitation whenever possible

Many sponsors do not appreciate being approached at events and trade shows by would-be endorsers of their product(s). Although they may want to meet you, these events are not set up for this sort of interaction. Unless you have made an appointment, or have been specifically asked to visit, do not work your resume at these events. Besides the fact that many sponsors do not want to be approached this way, your resume is likely to be misplaced or thrown away because they have no place to put it.

You can use these opportunities, however, to learn more about a company's products and to find out who to contact regarding sponsorship at a later date.

Always remember the bottom line is, "What can you do for the company?" If you remember this, your chances of getting sponsored will double.

SPONSORSHIP DON'TS STRAIGHT FROM THE SPONSORS' MOUTHS

"Don't wear out your welcome, don't get greedy."
— ALAN FOSTER, BICYCLE TEAM MANAGER, AIRWALK

"One thing that never receives consideration from us is a sponsorship request for money without any mention of product knowledge or acceptance. A sponsorship relationship is very risky with athletes who cannot demonstrate the ability to provide marketing value when representing a product or company. I receive many sponsorship requests from athletes who are highly competitive, want our money, but never even mention our product. These are probably form letters that are mass mailed."
— CHRIS POLSTER, CNS INC. (BREATHE RIGHT)

"Don't keep changing sponsors. We try to establish long-term relationships and if you keep jumping from one sponsor to another you lose credibility as a spokesperson."
— TAYA FRIEDMAN, SENIOR MARKETING ASSOCIATE, BRIKO

"Don't send a proposal that merely offers increased exposure in return for sponsorship. Though exposure is good, it is not enough to hook a sponsorship deal. If exposure is what you are offering, tell us how that exposure will lead to sales."
— TOM HILLARD, SPONSORSHIP DIRECTOR

"It's irritating when an athlete calls and asks for more money or product when the initial request was supposed to cover their needs. Companies have budgets that must be met and they like to know where they sit ahead of time. Little requests here and

there add up and can hurt an athlete's chances for obtaining sponsorship the next year."

— CHRIS CLINTON, SACHS BICYCLE COMPONENTS

"Most companies don't want to deal with racers at trade shows. The shows are for the manufacturers to show their products to dealers, make sales and answer dealer questions. Racers take time away from the dealers and cost the potential sponsor valuable time with their customers. Also, the quantity of resumes can create a logistical nightmare in the booth. Where do you put them where they won't get lost, written on, or thrown away?"

— CLINTON

CHAPTER five

NEGOTIATING YOUR DEAL

S ponsorship deals for professional athletes are often negotiated between the athlete's representative and the company's attorney or sponsorship representative. However, most sponsorship deals do not involve parties other than the athlete and the company representative. Negotiating a deal can place a lot of stress on an athlete who has absolutely no idea what he or she is doing. This chapter is designed to assist the athlete in the negotiation process and to provide some basic information about the different things that athletes can negotiate to receive.

If you get to the negotiation stage, the first thing to remember is to always be a polite, courteous, and good communicator. Be forthcoming with what you want out of the deal. Clearly state what your objectives are, and listen to the company's response. Many different situations exist at the negotiation stage. If your sponsorship is destined to be a product-only deal, then you really should not spend a lot of time trying to get money, because it probably will not happen. Plus, you may upset the person offering you free product, and he or she may withdraw the offer.

However, if your sponsorship has the potential to be a financial deal, then you should be prepared to negotiate. Depending on the extent of information that you provided in your proposal, you may have already placed a price tag on your deal. If this is the case, then it is up to the company to respond to the amount. If your proposal was vague and did not indicate a dollar figure, then either you will be asked during negotiations what you are looking for, or the company will start the bidding. Either way, your best chance for working out a deal is to negotiate fairly and honestly.

Remember, if an agreement is reached, you will be working to maintain a healthy, productive and positive relationship with the sponsor. Start right away by being honest and do not play hardball! You do not need to cave in and be vulnerable - but avoid using hard sales tactics to close the deal.

At the negotiating stage, it is very important to be professional and mature. The sponsor will take you seriously if you convey an attitude of professionalism. Sponsors are looking for good athletes and great spokespersons. Do not risk losing the sponsorship because you are a tough and unreasonable negotiator.

You can read terrific books on how to negotiate. When reading them, keep in mind that your situation is different from most of the examples given in the books. You are not negotiating the price of a new car that you are about to buy. In those negotiating situations, you can be as hard and rude as you want. You will not have a relationship with the car salesperson after the sale of the car.

The athlete-negotiator is a different breed than your average deal maker. You are not selling encyclopedias or vacuums, you are selling yourself. Your status as an athlete will determine how firm you can be with your wants and needs. If the company you are speaking with is your only option after sending out several proposals, then you need to be more flexible than if you were negotiating with several different interested companies.

Since you have most likely stated your opening position in your proposal, do not make greater demands during the negotiation stage. Your proposal will give the company an idea of what they may offer you. When it comes to products and discounts, take their offers at face value. There is really no room for counter offers or tactical negotiating at the beginner, novice, or lower expert categories. When any sort of financial arrangement is involved, counter offers and lengthier negotiations come into play.

If you are asked to interview with the company face-to-face, dress neatly, wear a smile, and offer a firm handshake. First impressions are very important.

Most athletes find it hard to negotiate for themselves. This is quite normal. An attorney, agent, or personal manager can be hired to facilitate the more complex negotiations.

FOR WHAT CAN YOU NEGOTIATE?

Remember the Sponsorship Diagram in Chapter 1?

Table 5-1: Sponsorship diagram

	CATEGORY 1	CATEGORY 2	CATEGORY 3	CATEGORY 4	CATEGORY 5
	Discounts	Free Products	Expenses Paid	Bonuses and Contingencies	Salaries
LEVEL 1	X				
LEVEL 2	X	X			
LEVEL 3	X	X	X		
LEVEL 4	X	X	X	X	
LEVEL 5	X	X	X	X	X

The top row describes different incentives to endorse a sponsor, items for which you can negotiate. The left column is the level of sponsorship corresponding to your abilities. Beginners and lower-end experts are usually negotiating at level 1 and level 2. High-end experts, elites, and lower-end pros are usually negotiating for level 3 and level 4. Level 5 is generally reserved for top professionals.

What Is the Extent to which Expenses are Paid?

A sponsor who supports an athlete by paying expenses normally includes travel (airfare, rental car), lodging, and a per diem for food. Some companies give a set amount of money for each venue and require you to budget your own expenses. Some companies make travel arrangements for you, others leave you in charge. These are details that will need to be worked out during the negotiation stage.

What Are Bonuses and Contingencies?

Bonuses and contingencies come in many forms and sizes. A company may agree to pay you a certain amount of money each time you place in the top ten, top five, or top three, at certain specified competitions. End-of-season overall title bonuses are fairly standard at level 4 and level 5. The extent of bonuses and contingencies should be addressed during negotiations and clearly set out in the sponsorship contract. You will need to know the following: (1) how much and when the sponsor will pay you for first, second, third, and so on, and (2) for which competitions the sponsor will pay. Table 5-2 provides a sample of a victory bonus schedule. Figures will vary depending on the sport and your level of competition.

Victory Bonus Schedule

Table 5-2: Victory Bonus Schedule

SPORT - BEACH VOLLEYBALL

	NATIONAL EVENTS	REGIONAL EVENTS
1ST	$1,000	$ 500
2ND	$ 750	$ 400
3RD	$ 500	$ 300
4TH	$ 250	$ 200
5TH	$ 150	$ 100

Note: All events must be pre-approved by sponsor for bonus schedule to apply.

There are also bonuses related to media exposure. Some companies will agree to pay media bonuses when a sponsored athlete is shown in a magazine, newspaper, or on television. Typically, the bonus is only paid when the sponsor's logo is clearly visible in the photo or on the television. The amount goes up as the coverage increases. Table 5-3 shows how a typical media bonus program works.

Media Bonus Schedule

Table 5-3: Example of a Media Bonus Schedule

PRINT	NATIONAL	LOCAL
1/4 page	$50	$25
1/2 page	$100	$50
Full page	$300	$100
Cover	$500	$200

TELEVISION	NATIONAL NETWORK	LOCAL NETWORK
Company name mentioned	$300	$150
Logo displayed	$500	$300

Some companies offer on-site sponsorship and product and/or cash bonuses to participating athletes. These programs, when available, are usually open to amateur competitors as well as professionals. In this type of program, the athlete is not officially sponsored by the company. The athlete has either purchased or been given the company's product. Then, at the competition site, sponsorship promoters have participating athletes sign a contract stating that they will be competing in the event using the company's product(s). If the athlete finishes in the top five, he or she gets a certain sum of money or free products. This sort of promotion-sponsorship is new, and companies that offer this type of promotion usually advertise the program in a trade magazine or event schedule. An amateur athlete certainly should not minimize the value of participating in such a program. Relationships can be built with the company by participating in these sorts of programs. Your participation will also show your dedication to the company and its products. The relationships that you build in the early years of your competition may help in the future when you are a professional seeking sponsorship.

One prominent company that offers this on-site type of sponsorship in the sport of bicycle racing is Sachs Bicycle Components. The photo below shows the area where athletes check-in at race venues in order to compete in the on-site promotion. Company spokesman Chris Clinton told us a bit about the program and how it works:

"We begin by advertising the on-site sponsorship in various trade magazines. When we arrive at an event, we set up a booth where athletes who are competing with our product(s) can sign up for sponsorship before the competition begins. First, the athlete has to come to the booth and show the technicians that he or she is using one or more of our products. Second, the athlete fills out a form that enters him or her into the Sachs Awards program. Third, we give the athlete a Sachs sticker or other promo-

tional item to place on his or her equipment during competition. Fourth, the athlete competes. If the athlete places within the parameters set by our agreement (which is usually a podium finish), he or she either gets an allotted cash amount or free product. This type of program can be quite beneficial to an athlete who participates consistently."

What about Salary?

Companies typically reserve salaried sponsorships for professional athletes. Athletes obtain the leverage to bargain for a salary once they have proven, by competition results, that they are among the best in the country or the world, or that they have the talent to be among the best.

The amount of salary such an athlete can demand depends on a few things. First, the athlete must consider his or her past performance and current world or national standings. The higher the athlete is in standings, the more money he or she can request. Next, the athlete must consider the nature of the sport and the amount of publicity it receives. If the sport is relatively large and is frequently highlighted in the media, a sponsor will be more interested in allocating marketing dollars to support an athlete, athletes, or a team. On the other hand, if the sport is small and receives little media coverage, a sponsor will be less likely to get involved so heavily.

Another consideration is the size of the company from which the athlete is seeking sponsorship. Smaller companies have less resources and therefore cannot pay out as much in sponsorship dollars as bigger companies. And, it is good to remember that just because a company is big (or appears to be big), that does not mean it has a large amount of money allocated to marketing, especially sports marketing.

Taking into consideration the individual sport, each athlete must decide whether to look for a single team sponsor, or for several independent sponsors.

DIFFERENT TYPES OF SPONSORSHIP

Team sponsorship is sponsorship by an already formed team. The team typically possesses its own sponsors and those sponsors become the team athlete's sponsors as well. Some athletes are not comfortable with someone else having control of sponsorhip this way. When this is the case, independent sponsorhip is a possible alternative.

Independent sponsorship is the situation where an athlete looks for his or her own sponsors individually.

Independent sponsorship is not limited to non-team members. An athlete who is part of a team can also obtain individual sponsors. However, the athlete must first obtain permission from the team manager and avoid direct conflicts with team sponsorships.

Combination sponsorship occurs when an athlete possesses both the team and individual sponsorship. This combination is ideal for gaining financial ground when money is involved. However, before pursuing this combination scenario, the athlete must make sure that team management knows of the desire for individual sponsors when such an opportunity arrives. The best time to discuss this is during the negotiation process.

So, when negotiating your deal, have a clear ideal of what you want to gain. Are you negotiating for discounts, or for a big salary? Are you negotiating with a team? If so, will you be able to obtain individual sponsors if such opportunities come your way? Then, once all the negotiating is done, it is time to secure the sponsorship agreement, as discussed in Chapter Six.

THE CONFUSING

WORLD OF CONTRACTS

T his chapter is not intended to offer legal advice to the reader. The main goal of this chapter is to provide the reader with some basic information about contracts. Since most athletes are not in a position to hire an attorney to look over contracts, these general self-help tips may be of assistance. If you have any doubt about your contract(s) or have questions, this is an area in which professional representation and/or consultation is advised. Never sign a contract unless you understand all the terms.

A contract is the legal obligation that results from the parties' agreement. Typically, it involves the exchange of promises between the parties. In sports sponsorship, contracts can be written or oral. Contrary to what most people think, oral contracts can be valid. Validity depends on the specific circumstances of the situation, so if you feel as if a sponsor is in breach of an oral contract (and there is money involved), it may be a good idea to consult an attorney to find out whether you have a claim for damages.

If a sponsor offers a deal and requests that it remain oral and not formalized, then you need to use your best judgment. If you are weary and have other offers waiting for a reply, then you may want to consider taking the best written deal, because the best contract is a written contract. In some sports, sponsors do not provide a written sponsorship agreement unless asked, while others make certain that every agreement is signed and formally executed. It is important to have sponsorship deals in writing, and they should be signed by the company decision-maker. Not only does a written document provide protection for the athlete, it is also provides protection for the company. Without a written agreement, it will be difficult to resolve any disagreement which may arise out of the sponsorship relationship.

Always make sure that you have a copy of the sponsorship contract with all the required signatures and keep it in a safe place. This is for your protection. Also, you may need to use your copy as a reference throughout the contractual term.

Contracts longer than one page should be numbered at the bottom in a specific format. For example, if a contract is four pages long, the pages should be numbered as follows: 1 of 4, 2 of 4, 3 of 4, and 4 of 4. This is for both your and the company's protection. Refer to the sample sponsorship agreement in Appendix K.

It may be a good idea to hire an attorney or an athlete manager to look over your contract(s) before signing – especially when money is involved. Getting sponsored is an exciting time, but you need to be patient. The first contract that the company sends to you is not necessarily the final draft. Changes can always be made before you sign.

QUICK TIPS

- Get It In Writing
- Make a Copy
- Protect Your Rights
- Make Sure the Contract Is Numbered Correctly
- Get a Signature From the Company Decision-Maker
- Follow Through On Your Part Of the Deal

CHAPTER seven

ALTERNATIVES TO

SPONSORSHIP

I f you are someone who is new in your sport, interested in finding bargains, or cannot afford competitive products and wish you could, this chapter will help you. It is an introduction to sponsorship alternatives and other ways to get great deals.

Here are six alternatives to sponsorship:

- Pro deals
- Local "B" teams or farm teams
- On-site sponsorship programs
- The bulletin board at the sports shop
- Newspaper and magazine classifieds
- Local professional athlete

PRO DEALS

Occasionally, sponsors offer what is commonly known as a pro deal to athletes that send in their resumes requesting sponsorship. A pro deal is akin to sponsorship in that it provides the athlete with a significant discount on competition equipment (usually wholesale cost). And, as part of the deal, the company usually provides competition clothing with its logo for the athlete to wear when competing.

When a company offers you a pro deal your first instinct may be to blow it off as insulting. But, this is not an insult and should be considered as an offer for sponsorship and treated with as much respect. Most companies do not and cannot offer pro deals to every athlete who sends in a proposal. They carefully weed through the resumes that are sent to them and pick only those that are qualified to receive a pro deal. The main reason why all athletes do not receive these offers is because companies cannot undersell their distributors too often. So, depending on your status as an athlete, you should consider pro deals as a way of working your way up the sponsorship ladder.

"B" Teams or Farm Teams

If you are actually competing on a regular basis, you may be eligible to participate in what companies and sport shops typ-

Peggy Welch, M2 Images

MANY SPORT SHOPS HAVE TEAMS OR PROGRAMS THAT SUPPORT LOCAL ATHLETES AND LOCAL COMPETITION.

ically call "B" teams or farm teams. These teams are made up of athletes who compete in certain geographical areas. For example, if you live in Northern California, you may be able to find a sport shop or professional team that has a farm team in your area. Once you are able to track down such a team, you should follow the proposal structure as described in this book.

Farm teams normally provide athletes with products at wholesale (or below wholesale) prices and training/competition clothing with sponsor's logos. Occasionally, you can find a farm team that will offer to pay for your entry fees or offer bonuses for certain victories. Each business/shop is different. Look into several options before making a commitment to one team. The team will most likely require that you compete in a certain number of events during the season in return for its sponsorship. Whatever the arrangement, this type of sponsorship is just as special as any other — treat the sponsor and its product with respect and dignity.

On-Site Sponsorship Programs

On-site sponsorship programs were discussed in detail in Chapter 5. To refresh your memory, some companies offer on-site sponsorship programs at competition venues in which any athlete can participate. Typically, the company sets up a booth where athletes who are competing with that company's product(s) can sign up for sponsorship before the competition begins. First, the athlete goes to the booth and shows the technicians that he or she is using the company's products. Second, the athlete fills out a form that enters him or her into the program. Third, the company gives the athlete a company sticker or other promotional item to place on the equipment during competition. Fourth, the athlete competes. If the athlete places within the parameters set by the agreement, he or she either gets an allotted cash amount or free product. This type of program can be quite beneficial to an athlete who participates consistently.

SACHS AWARDS PROGRAM & SPONSORSHIP GURU CHRIS CLINTON.

THE BULLETIN BOARD AT THE SPORTS SHOP

Most sports shops have bulletin boards, where people are trying to sell their used equipment. Most of these sellers either never used the product, or want to upgrade. They are usually eager to sell. This means that if you can offer them cash, you may be able get the product below their asking price. Sellers usually do not go through the trouble of putting up signs unless it is a good product. So keep looking at the board, huge bargains can be found.

NEWSPAPER AND MAGAZINE CLASSIFIEDS

This concept is similar to the bulletinboard described above. However, now the seller is actually paying money to sell his or her product. This means the seller is extremely motivated.

Many of these sellers rarely used the product; therefore, it should be in good condition. Only pick those ads that are selling one or two items. A classified ad that lists 10 different items for sale makes it less likely that the quality of the product is top notch.

Your Local Professional Athlete

If there is a professional athlete in your area, you could be in luck. Professionals receive new product annually. What do you think happens to the products left over from last season? Many times products you would "die for" sit in the garage unused. Many professionals have so much extra product that they do not know what to do with it. Find a local shop that works with the athlete. Leave your name and number with the shop and explain that you are interested in any products or equipment the pro is no longer using. The athlete will call if he or she is interested in getting rid of items.

CHAPTER eight

WHO NEEDS A MANAGER?

Not every athlete needs a business manager or an agent. Managers and agents typically reserve their services for professionals or exceptional amateurs who are ready to make the transition to the professional ranks.

A business manager can help you with everything from creating your proposal, to closing the final deals, to financial planning. The extent of the business relationship should be dictated by what you need and what the manager has to offer. Some sports management companies offer legal and financial services in addition to the typically offered sponsor targeting, athlete placement, and contract negotiations.

If you are an athlete who needs a manger, you will have to decide which services you need and then find a manager/agent who offers those services. Keep in mind that several states have enacted laws that protect the athlete from unqualified representation.

You should question the competence and qualifications of a prospective manager before you sign an athlete-agent agreement. Ask to see a list of other athletes the firm represents and read any client testimonials that are available. Managers who are also attorneys are likely to meet the legal standards in your state. Attorneys are held to an ethical standard that requires them to avoid conflicts of interest and to zealously represent their clients. If the manager is not an attorney, your state may require that he or she become a state-certified athlete agent. Table 8-1 provides you with the contact information for current athlete-agent legislation in your state. As athlete-agent regulation is relatively new, some states had not enacted laws at the time this book went to print. If the state you live in is not listed, you should contact the Secretary of State's office or the Attorney General's office in your state to find out if any recent legislation has been enacted.

Table 8-1: Where to Obtain Your State's Current Athlete-Agent Legislation.

STATE	WHERE TO OBTAIN CURRENT INFORMATION
AL	Alabama Athlete Agent Regulatory Commttee Secretary of State Alabama State Capital Building Room E210 300 Dexter Ave. Montgomery, AL 36103-5616 (334) 242-7591 contact: Sharon Frith
AR	Secretary of State Arkansas State Capital Little Rock, AR 72201 (501) 682-5070 contact: Kathleen McQueen
AZ	Contact Arizona Secretary of State (602) 542-4285
CA	California Secretary of State Sacramento, CA (916) 653-6814

CT	Connecticut General Assembly Office of Legislative Research Room 5300 Hartford, CT 06106 (860) 240-8400
FL	Florida Dept. of Business & Professional Regulations Division of Professions, Athlete Agents Northwood Center 1940 North Monroe Street Tallahassee, FL 32399-0774 (850) 922-8981
GA	State Examining Board Georgia Athlete Agent Regulatory Commission 166 Pryor Street S.W. Atlanta, GA 30303 (404) 656-6719
IN	Legislative Services Agency 302 State House Indianapolis, IN 46204 (317) 232-9856
IA	Iowa Secretary of State Athlete Agent Registration Hoover Building, 2nd Floor Des Moines, Iowa 50319 (515) 281-5204
KY	Legislative Research Commission Capital Building, 4th Floor Frankfort, KY 40601 (502) 564-8100
LA	Louisiana Secretary of State Corporations Division P.O. Box 94125 Baton Rouge, LA 70804-9125 (504) 925-4704
MA	Massachusetts Secretary of State (617) 727-7030 information line
MD	Maryland Secretary of State (410) 767-6314 Contact: Rhonda Ray, Legislative Liason
MN	Minnesota Secretary of State 100 Constitution Avenue State Office Building, Room 180 St. Paul, MN 55155 (612) 296-6013 (612) 296-2146 House info line (612) 296-0504 Senate info line

MS	Mississippi Secretary of State P.O. Box 136 Jackson, MS 39205 (601) 359-1604 Contact: Ray Bailey
NE	Contact Nebraska Secretary of State (402) 471-2554
NV	Nevada Secretary of State Carson City, NV (702) 687-5203
NC	North Carolina Department of the Secretary of State 300 North Salisbury Street Raleigh, NC 27603 (919) 733-3924
ND	Secretary of State Bismark, ND (701) 328-2900
OH	Ohio State House Legislative Info line Columbus, OH (614) 466-8842, (800) 282-0253
OK	Oklahoma Secretary of State Filings Department 2300 North Lincoln Blvd., Room 101 Oklahoma City, OK 73105 (405) 522-4560
OR	Contact Oregon Secretary of State (503) 986-1500
PA	Pennsylvania State Athletic Commission 116 Pine St. Third Floor Harrisburg, PA 17101 (717) 787-5720
SC	Contact: Greg Sirb South Carolina Department of Consumer Affairs P.O. Box 5757 Columbia, SC 29250 (803) 734-9461
TN	Tennessee Office of the Attorney General 450 James Robertson Parkway Nashville, TN 37243 (615) 741-3491
TX	Texas Secretary of State Statutory Documents Section P.O. Box 12887 Austin, TX 78711 (512) 475-1769 Contact: Dorothy Wilson

WA	Washington State Department of Licensing Professional Athletics Athlete Agents Office P.O. Box 9649 Olympia, WA 98507 (360) 753-3713 Contact: Michael Recor

When negotiating a business management contract, you should never contract away more than ten percent of your gross income. Some states allow for more than ten percent, but most limit the amount to the former. The amount that you pay your manager is negotiable and should be addressed in detail during the negotiation process. You may also be required to reimburse the manger for expenses (such as telephone calls, faxes, and postage) that are spent on your behalf. It is a good idea to set a yearly budget with the manager so that you do not get stuck with a huge bill. Be sure that your agreement states when you will be billed for services rendered (i.e., once a month or bimonthly) and when you are expected to pay (i.e., within thirty days). Clearly identifying the scope of your business relationship from the beginning will help develop a positive relationship. Put everything in writing. (See the Sample Agent-Athlete Agreement in Appendix J.)

Some things that an agent or manager may do for the athlete include:

• Solicit endorsement contracts and sponsorships
• Solicit for personal appearances
• Arrange promotional events
• Establish relations with the media on behalf of the athlete
• Attend press conferences
• Prepare written speeches
• Handle financial and/or legal affairs

• Arrange for income tax preparation

• Plan for athlete's post-career

Lastly, it is very important that you keep in close contact with your manager once you sign an agreement. Keep him or her informed of any new developments in your career and be sure to pass on any leads that you come across. Never do anything behind the back of your manager. You want to appear to the public as a team. Always be candid and truthful. This relationship can make or break you, YOU MUST DO YOUR BEST TO ESTABLISH GREAT RAPPORT.

CHAPTER NINE

MARKETING
a SPORTS TEAM

This chapter is for those of you in charge of developing a sponsorship program for an entire team or large program. Whether you are the team manager reporting to a world-class company or an ambitious person desiring to start your own team from scratch, team sponsorships are obtained through a process similar to the individual athlete process discussed in chapter 2. However, the team sponsorship step-by-step process will take more time, more money, and a specific business proposal format.

The following is the outline of the step-by-step process for getting team sponsorship:

STEP 1: Determine your team program objectives

STEP 2: Make a contact list and do the research

STEP 3: Establish a team budget

STEP 4: Develop your sponsorship proposal

STEP 5: Send the proposals

STEP 6: Do the necessary follow-ups

STEP 7: Send thank you letters and keep sponsors informed

STEP 1:

DETERMINE YOUR TEAM PROGRAM OBJECTIVES

First you will need to determine your overall team goals. Then answer some of the following questions.

DO I ALREADY HAVE FINANCIAL BACKING TO START THE TEAM?

Most teams are developed by a company or a willing investor that has enough financial resources to start a minimal team program. Your job as the team manager is to enhance the team program by obtaining additional sponsorship dollars. If you do not have an initial financial base, starting a team will be tough. Finding that one company or person with resources should be your first priority. Initial funding is usually obtained through contacts you already have. Rarely is the initial financial backing from a company or person that does not know you or your company personally.

DOES MY TEAM ALREADY HAVE ATHLETES?

Do you already have the national champion or potential world champion willing to be listed on your team roster? Or, do you not have athletes for the program and plan to acquire them once you find team sponsorship dollars? This is an important factor when putting your proposal together. If the actual team members are already known, selling them along with your program may help secure sponsorships.

WILL TEAM ATHLETES BE PROFESSIONALS, AMATEURS, OR BOTH?

Companies want to know what level of competitors they will

Mark Doolittle, Fat Tire Fotos

DETERMINE THE SIZE OF YOUR TEAM EARLY IN THE PROPOSAL PROCESS. DOES YOUR TEAM INCLUDE ONE RIDER OR MANY?

be supporting. Will the athletes be top professionals that travel worldwide, or will they be amateur athletes racing regionally at a beginner level? Or, will your team roster represent both sides of athletic competition, amateur and professional? Companies want to know details, so be sure to work these issues out before you start contacting potential sponsors.

WHAT KIND OF EXPOSURE CAN MY SPORT OFFER A COMPANY?

The level of media exposure that your sport receives and kind of demographics it reaches will be an important factor when a potential sponsor is deciding whether or not to get involved. Companies want to know how much exposure they will receive by becoming involved with this particular sport. As stated elsewhere in this book, companies get hundreds of requests for sponsorship from all sorts of sports enthusiasts, you must show the reader of the sponsorship request why your sport and your program are the best in which to get involved.

WHAT TEAM PROGRAMS AND PROMOTIONS WILL OFFER EXTRA EXPOSURE FOR SPONSORS?

Besides the use of the sponsor's product or its logo placement on the team uniform, what other exposure can you offer the sponsor in return for sponsorship? You can offer potential sponsors the placement of their logos on team vehicles, exposition tents, and in advertising campaigns. Always think of every possible avenue to increase exposure opportunities for your potential sponsors. Extra exposure leads to sales — your potential sponsor's main goal.

WHAT LEVELS OF SPONSORSHIP DO I NEED TO OFFER IN ORDER TO MEET PROGRAM BUDGETS?

A team costs money — potential sponsors know this fact. What levels of sponsorship you offer depends on your team budget. You will need to present your sponsorship request in a fashion that is easy for the company to understand. Step 3 below discusses this concept in detail.

HAS MY TEAM/PROGRAM BEEN AROUND FOR YEARS, OR IS THIS A TEAM STARTING FROM SCRATCH?

If your team or company has been around for years and has a positive reputation, convincing a sponsor of your potential for future success will be much easier than if you represent a rookie team with no roots. If you are managing a newly formed team, try to create an angle that is unique and sell that concept. The unique stature of the team may be enough to compensate for the fact that the team is just a newborn.

Having a good understanding of your objectives is very important. These are only a few questions that could pertain to any sport. Make sure that you also think through the logistics of your particular sport.

STEP 2:

MAKE A CONTACT LIST AND DO THE RESEARCH

Once you understand your objectives, you need to begin the research phase of the STEP-by-STEP process. Begin by making a list of the companies that you would like to contact and do some simple research.

MAKE A CONTACT LIST

Make a list of all the products and companies that you would like your team to endorse. Look through magazines, watch television commercials, visit local sports shops, go to vendor booths at sports events and attend industry trade shows to get ideas. Watch sports events on television and look for company banners in the background.

FIND THE PHONE NUMBERS AND ADDRESSES

Once you have made your contact list, find the telephone numbers and addresses of each company. Try to find toll-free numbers as often as possible. Remember, however, that some companies intend that their toll-free numbers be used exclusively for sales. If the receptionist asks you to call a direct line, do it. And, you want to be sure that you obtain the correct mailing address of each company so that you can ensure the proposals arrive safely.

One way to get this information about the companies is to look each of them up on the Internet. Also, you can often send e-mail to a company, ask questions and receive a timely response. Or, you can use the old-fashioned approach and call them on the phone.

CALL EACH COMPANY

You should call each company and say to the first person who answers the phone, "Hi. Can you please tell me who to contact regarding sports sponsorship." Make sure you ask for the proper spelling of the contact person's name. Next, ask for the address, if you do not have it, or confirm the address that you do have. This initial phone call should last no longer than two or three minutes. Do not attempt to talk to the sponsorship contact at this time and do not indentify yourself. If the receptionist puts you through to the contact, briefly state your interest in the company and let him or her know that you will be sending in a proposal.

Occasionally the receptionist or sponsorship coordinator will ask you to fax your proposal. Try to avoid sending team sponsorship proposals by fax. A team sponsorship proposal needs to be as impressive as possible, and a faxed document is not impressive. Instead, if your contact needs it in a hurry, tell him or her you will send it overnight via an expedited mail service.

Now that you have your contact list, the addresses, and the contact people, it is time to establish your team budget.

STEP 3:

Establish A Team Budget

Budgeting for the Proposal Process

The team proposal process can be significantly more expensive than the individual process. The process described herein is based on the assumption you are interested in obtaining extensive funding from a corporate sponsor. Asking for big dollars means that you should make your proposal an official business proposal. Official business proposals have a specific format, and are usually between eight to twenty pages long. And, if you want to find a corporate sponsor, sometimes you will send hundreds of proposals before you even get a response. Budgeting anywhere from $500 to $3,000 is typical due to the following necessities: hiring a computer designer/artist, purchasing high quality materials, mass quantity printing, quality binding, sending big folders first class, and miscellaneous costs. So, prepare your proposal budget before you start the STEP-by-STEP process. Generating a budget will be easier to do once you review the proposal format in Step 4. See Appendix A for a proposal budget worksheet.

Budgeting for Competition

Travel expenses for an entire team can be extremely expensive. These expenses are gauged primarily by the number of athletes on the team and the extent of the team program. However, it is not just athletes you have to consider. If you are developing a team program, you will have to decide whether you need to hire additional team members such as a team manager, team vehicle driver, mechanics, assistants, masseuse, and administrative people.

Some items to consider when figuring your team budget are:

- Entry fees (for all competitors)
- Travel expenses (for all competitors and team crew)
- Lodging/hotel accommodations
- Airfare
- Rental cars
- Food allowance
- Exposition registration fees/parking (for each event)
- Team travel vehicles, maintenance and insurance
- Athlete salaries, victory bonuses
- Team crew salaries
- Competition equipment
- Competition clothing
- Publicity costs (media contact, advertising, sponsor newsletters)
- Other administrative costs

STEP 4:

DEVELOP YOUR SPONSORSHIP PROPOSAL

Developing the team proposal is the most time consuming part of the sponsorship project. If you are soliciting corporate sponsors for large sums of money, your proposal should be in a specific, professional proposal format. Remember, not only will your proposal be selling your team, it will be selling your whole program, and your sport. A complete proposal should include the following:

- Front cover
- Table of contents
- Executive summary

- Information about your sport
- Proposed programs and promotions
- Your company's history and/or product description
- Team overview
- Team budget
- Sponsorship levels
- Visual aids for logo placements
- Venue list
- Contacts
- Cover letter

If your proposal budget does not allow for all of the items above, include the essential items such as cover letter, the proposed program and promotion, information on the team members, venue list and sponsorship levels. A team proposal can be complete with just these items, but if you can afford to include all the items in your proposal, do it. Keep in mind, however, that if you are soliciting sponsorship from sports companies within your sport, the team proposal does not have to include all of the items mentioned above. You can safely assume that if a company is already involved in sponsorship within the sport, decision makers already know the sport's demographics.

FRONT COVER

If you can afford the expense, the team proposal should be professionally bound and approximately eight to twenty pages long. A front cover is very important because it is the first thing that the company will see. It should be simple, yet pleasing to the eye. Make sure the front cover states that the document is a sponsorship proposal for your particular sport. Consider having a color photo or graphics on the front. Be creative, but do not overdo it. Remember that clean, professional simplicity goes a long way. Too many graphics and bright colors can be distracting, not to mention a turn-off, to the reader.

TABLE OF CONTENTS

The contents page provides the reader with a brief overview of the proposal. Thus, it helps the reader understand the proposal and locate specific sections quickly. Put the heading of the section on the left, and the corresponding page number on the right as depicted in Table 9-1.

In addition to the actual proposal contents, insert your contact information (name, address, telephone number, fax, and e-mail) at the bottom of the page. It is important to have this contact information in several places so that the company representative can find it easily when he or she is ready to call. You should also put this information on the last page of the proposal, and in the cover letter.

Table 9-1: Example of Contents Page for the Team Proposal

CONTENTS

Executive Summary	1
The Sport	2
Team Programs	3
Sponsorship Levels	4
Race Venue List	5
Contacts	6

EXECUTIVE SUMMARY

Positioned on page one, the executive summary explains the essential elements of the entire proposal. This overview simplifies the reader's understanding of a long proposal. Because of the increased volume of information that mangers must review, the tendency in business today is for mangers to require an executive summary regardless of the length and complexity of a report or proposal.

The executive summary should briefly introduce the purpose of the proposal and summarize the major sections of the proposal. It should have its own page following the table of contents and be strictly limited to one page.

Information About the Sport

If you solicit companies in industries outside your sport, they will want to know about the sport that you are asking them to sponsor. The history, current status, and demographics of the sport should be discussed in the proposal.

When discussing the history of your sport, avoid boring the reader. Be brief. Hit the highlights and move on to the sport's current status, growth, and demographics. If you are writing to a sponsor whose industry is associated with your sport, these demographics may not be necessary. These companies already are well-equipped with this sort of information.

Call up your sports director or national organization and ask for a current press kit detailing the sport's demographics. Potential sponsors want to know details about the market the particular sport serves; current demographics will provide this information. Sports sponsorship is only one way that businesses employ their marketing dollars. Companies want to make sure they are spending their money wisely by advertising to the correct market: the right age group, the right income bracket, the right number of people, and so on. If you can, use graphics to display this information. Bar graphs and pie charts work especially well.

Programs and Promotions

During the "what are your objectives?" step, programs and promotions should have been created. What kind of program do you have or are you planning to have and how will the potential sponsors benefit? How will sponsoring your team lead to exposure and an increase in sales? Will your program have a big travel vehicle, exposition tents, and athletes at all the competitions? Will your program have an advertising campaign? Will you have top professional athletes that travel worldwide or nationally? These are the things that potential sponsors want to know.

In essence, describe your program. Tell the potential sponsor all the details of the program and how their company will benefit (key phrase: "increased sales"). Do it in an organized fashion, and be direct.

History of Your Company, Product, or Team

If you are the manager of an established team or company, give a brief history of your proven success. Use a color photo to help the potential sponsor visualize your product, company, or team. If your team or product somehow relates to the potential sponsor's product(s), establish that connection in this section. If you are creating a new team program, briefly state why you are doing so and what you hope to accomplish. For example, a few years back an all-woman mountain bike team was established. Their primary goal was to create more opportunities for women in the sport. If you are starting a new team, consider finding a niche to help sell your program to potential sponsors.

The Team

If you are lucky enough to already have athletes committed

to your program, reserve a page in your proposal to describe them. If there are too many athletes to describe, highlight the stars and list the others briefly. Do not write out each athlete's entire resume. Only hit a few impressive highlights in each athlete's career. Consider including a photograph of each athlete in this section for emphasis.

YOUR BUDGET

You should have already figured your budget in Step 3. Now, try to develop some sort of graph or table for the budget page. Be creative. A simple table might just have a column for the expense, and a column for the funding needed for that particular expense, as seen in Table 9-2.

Table 9-2: Team Budget Example

TEAM BUDGET

Travel Expenses	$ 60,000
Athlete Salaries	$100,000
Marketing	$ 30,000
Team Vehicles	$ 25,000
TOTAL BUDGET	**$215,000**

A visual presentation of the team budget gives the potential sponsor an explanation of where the sponsorship money will be spent. Table 9-2 is only an example of a team budget. Do not let the dollar amounts or the format scare you. Your team budget may be much lower or much higher depending on the scope of your program.

SPONSORSHIP LEVELS

Your request for specific sponsorship dollars should come in the form of tiered sponsorship levels. When you establish different levels of sponsorship, you give potential sponsors choices of how to spend their marketing dollars. As each level increases in marketing exposure, so does the cost of its corresponding sponsorship.

Levels of sponsorship are usually given titles with a sense of hierarchy. For example, sponsorship levels have been called the following:

- Gold, silver, bronze, platinum
- Supreme, premium, regular
- Title sponsor, co-title sponsor, co- sponsor, support sponsor
- Partner, associate, entry level
- Primary, secondary, associate

Be creative when naming your sponsorship levels. Present the potential sponsor with something unique and fresh.

A dollar amount must correspond to each level of sponsorship. This book cannot tell you how to price your levels. Your budget will determine the amount at which you must price your levels. One team's gold level may be $1,000,000, while another team may establish the gold level at $1,000. It is all relative to the size and scope of your program.

Next, each level must be accompanied by a list of sponsor benefits. Maximum exposure benefits will correspond to the highest level, while the minimum amount of exposure will correspond with the lowest sponsorship level. Table 9-3 shows the relation between dollar amount and benefits.

VISUAL AIDS

Using drawings or pictures to illustrate where potential sponsor's logos will appear in your team program is extremely important. If you use gold, silver, and bronze as your sponsorship levels, a computerized drawing of your team uniform,

Table 9-3: Sponsorship levels and benefits

Sponsorship Levels and Corresponding Benefits

GOLD - $10,000

- Largest logo on uniform (specify size - 8" x 4")
- Largest logo on vehicle
- Use of product in all competitions
- Company can use name and likeness of team athletes for marketing

SILVER - $5,000

- Medium logo on uniform
- Medium logo on vehicle
- Use of product in all competitions
- Company can use name and likeness of team athletes for marketing

BRONZE - $2,500

- Small logo on uniform
- Use of product in all competitions
- Company can use name and likeness of team athletes for marketing

with gold, silver, bronze in their respective spaces and sizes will help the company visualize its potential exposure.

Other drawings could include those marketing tools visible to the public such as team vehicles and tents. Visual aids help the reader evaluate the scope of the program and its value to potential sponsors. While visual aids are not necessary, they help demonstrate your ideas to the person reading the proposal.

COMPETITION VENUES

Include a competition venue list for the company. Potential sponsors always want to know the scope and duration of your program. Occasionally, sponsors determine which teams they'll support based on which venues - and markets - the team will visit. See the sample competition-venue schedule in Chapter 2 and the competition-venue worksheet in Appendix F for an idea of how to put this list together.

CONTACTS

Your proposal should include one or two people that potential sponsors can contact to discuss the contents of the proposal. The contact person or people should be authorized to discuss the proposal, negotiate contract terms, and close final deals. Do not waste the potential sponsor's time by running him or her through your own hierarchy of contacts.

You should list the name(s) of the contact(s) at the bottom of the contents page and on a separate page reserved for contact information. You should include the contact's name, title, phone number, fax number, and address. If the contact has an e-mail address, be sure to include that as well.

COVER LETTER

When sending team proposals use the same cover letter format as for an individual sponsorship (see chapter 2). The main difference when you solicit corporate sponsors outside of your sports industry is that your cover letter should briefly explain how their product relates to your sport. Putting this information in the second or third paragraph is best.

The next thing you will have to decide is whether the cover letter will be bound within the proposal or kept outside the bound proposal. Both methods are acceptable; however, a cover letter outside the bound proposal is definitely best. This way you can personalize the cover letter to each company. A cover letter addressed directly to the person in charge, including knowledge about the company's specifics, and relating these specifics to your sport is much more effective than a form letter. A cover letter designed inside the proposal addressing "To Whom It May Concern" will only waste time and money because you are not likely to receive a response. Be personal.

Mass produce the proposal, but make sure you personalize the cover letter.

If you only send a few proposals, customize each one for the company to which you send it. This method, however, is not recommended if you are trying to produce a number of professional reports under time constraints. A personalized cover letter is usually enough to show that you are interested in a specific company's product and have taken the time to do some basic research.

STEP 5:

Send The Proposal

Putting the Elements Together

Put the cover letter on top of the proposal. Insert them neatly into an envelope that fits snugly. A 9x12 envelope usually will be sufficient. You can paper clip the cover letter to the proposal, or leave it loose. If applicable, attach your business card to the cover letter, again giving them the contact information.

Getting It Out the Door

Once you have all your proposals stuffed, sealed, and addressed, go to the post office to mail them. Request first class postage for all of the proposals. If you have the budget, send your proposals via some expedited delivery service (Express Mail, UPS, or Federal Express). This way you will also have some sort of receipt and will be able to account for delivery.

STEP 6:

FOLLOW UP

After you have sent your proposal(s), wait approximately two weeks for a response. If you do not hear from the company, follow up with a phone call asking for the person to whom you sent the proposal. If you are unable to contact this person by phone, write a brief follow-up letter stating your continued interest in the company/product. Remind him or her of the proposal you sent and your excitement in hearing back from them. (For an example of a follow-up letter, see Appendix E).

STEP 7:

SEND A THANK YOU LETTER
AND KEEP SPONSORS INFORMED

Whether you were rejected right away, or signed a deal, always send a short thank you for the company's response and let them know that you will try again next year or that you are looking forward to working with them. This shows your respect for the company and improves your chances of being remembered when you submit a proposal next year. You should also send your sponsor(s) an occasional handwritten thank you when they send product on time or do something else that you really appreciate. (For an example of thank you letters, see Appendix E).

If you made a deal with a sponsor, one of the most important things to do during the term of the sponsorship is to keep them informed of your progress. Most sponsors really want to hear from the athletes that they provide money and/or product to and will value your updates. One of the best ways to keep sponsors informed is with a newsletter or press release. These updates do not have to be personalized to each sponsor, but they should be directed to your sponsors generally. A sample newsletter worksheet can be found in Appendix H. One complaint which is frequently heard from companies is that the teams they sponsor do not stay in touch after they receive the money or products. A great way to show your appreciation and respect for the company is to keep them informed (even if the news isn't so hot).

CHAPTER ten

MARKETING A SPORTING EVENT

E vent marketing provides companies with an opportunity for more individualized exposure. The sponsorship of sports events ranges from local little leagues to the Olympic Games. Accordingly, companies can get involved with local event sponsorships for a nominal amount or with national event sponsorships with substantial price tags. Events provide sports marketers with a wide range of options.

It is important to remember that most companies are already bombarded with proposals. The goal of the event organizer should be to present something innovative. With the growing deluge of extreme and alternative sports, the event coordinator should strive to establish an event that is not only unique, but has the ability to adapt to changing times. Ultimately, the goals of the event coordinator should be to create a sponsorship package that is both unique and affordable.

The main reason that event coordinators offer sponsorships is to generate funds to conduct the event, because sport events cost a lot of money to produce. Many events sell tickets to spectators to raise revenue. An innovative event coordinator will develop a sponsorship strategy that is advantageous to both the event and its sponsors.

Some ways to accomplish this task are to:

- Make the sponsorship opportunities affordable, yet exclusive
- Make sure the event location is large enough to accommodate competitors, spectators, and media crews.
- Be sure that sponsorships include perks such as VIP parking, VIP event passes, and VIP events.
- Offer sponsors and their guests an opportunity to mingle with elite athletes at a dinner, lunch, or cocktail function sometime during the event.
- Think of an event concept that has never been done before (or is done infrequently) that will ensure competitor, spectator, and media interest.
- Contact the media as soon as you have developed your concept. Use press packets, press releases, or newsletters.
- Bring in media sponsors - to ensure media coverage of the event.

Some of the things a sports marketer will consider when deciding whether to sponsor an event are:

1. Its affordability
2. The overall image of the event
3. The event's target market
4. Cross-marketing opportunities
5. The total amount of guaranteed exposure
6. Overall value

Creating an event is not an easy task. Getting sponsors for the event is even tougher. The overall marketing scheme which the event coordinator should follow is the basic step-by-step

William E. Drury, 1997

EXAMPLE OF SPORTS EVENT SPONSORSHIP. VISA AND TEAM BIG BEAR ARE OBVIOUS SPONSORS OF THIS EVENT.

process outlined and discussed in chapters 2 and 9. The event coordinator can develop these materials or hire a professional to do the work.

Both sports company and non-sports company sponsors should be sought. The main reason for this is that you will probably have to offer exclusivity in order to sell an event sponsorship, and this will limit your prospects early on. Additionally, event coordinators should make a good faith effort to offer community tie-in sponsorships. A community tie-in sponsorship is an opportunity directed at local businesses such as hotels, restaurants, and sports shops. These types of sponsorships should be considered as cross-marketing opportunities for the event coordinator. A hotel, for example, will agree to offer rooms at a reduced rate to competitors and spectators in return for recognition as the event's host hotel. Flyers and registration forms would include information about the host hotel, and participants would most likely make reservations there. The community tie-in has several benefits: it fosters good will in the community in which the event is taking place; it provides discounts to registrants and spectators (which may encourage attendance); it puts money back into the community; and it increases the event's appearance as a legitimate event.

This chapter is not everything you need to know about event marketing. However, it should get you started, and the step-by-step process should help you create a professional event marketing package.

CHAPTER eleven

DEALING WITH THE MEDIA AND OTHER SELF-PROMOTIONS

W hether you are an individual athlete, manager of a team, or an event coordinator, you need to become familiar with the nuances of promotions and interacting with the media. Broadly speaking, the media includes two categories, print and electronic. Print media is generally newspapers and magazines. Electronic media includes television and radio. New technology, such as the Internet, combines both print and electronic media characteristics and is nearly as important as the other two. This chapter briefly discusses some techniques for interacting with the media and offers suggestions from media experts. This chapter also discusses fan appreciation as a way to positively promote yourself, your team, or your event.

In order to effectively promote yourself, your team, or your event, you need to become familiar with all the different media outlets. If one of your goals is to establish media contacts, you must take the time to develop some basic skills and nurture productive relationships with members of the media. Besides

William E. Drury

**AS A PROFESSIONAL ATHLETE, FAN AND MEDIA ATTENTION IS REALLY
IMPORTANT.**

paid advertising, you can obtain media exposure through publicity, most notably over newsworthy stories.

One piece of advice to the competitive athlete or team manager is not to contact the media unless you have a newsworthy story. If you are an athlete without a newsworthy story, but really want to see your name in lights, then you have to create something that your community (local or national) will be interested in knowing about you. The main reason you want to avoid contacting members of the media before you have a newsworthy story is that they will not be interested. They may even become angry if you waste their time. This is not to say that the media is mean or snobby. Its members are simply very busy people with hectic schedules and not a lot of time to spare.

How do you create a newsworthy story? Well, the best place to start is by giving something back to your community. Community interest stories always attract the media. For example, if you are an amateur volleyball player, you may consider putting on a volleyball training camp for beginners, up-and-coming players, youths, or handicapped people. If you choose to put on such an event, be creative and invite the media to participate for free. Then, have press packets (as discussed below) available. If you are a hometown hero (i.e., someone who has already established a positive presence in the community), you might arrange to sign autographs in a local sports shop. If you are a professional athlete, you have a duty to be a community role model and events such as this are newsworthy. Don't limit yourself to these suggestions: there are dozens of things that you can do to generate community and media interest in your endeavors. Be creative.

Before you begin dealing with the media on any level, however, it would be wise to establish your media network. Take some time to establish media contacts. The key word here is time, do not force relationships.

Establishing Your Media Network

The first thing you have to do is determine the scope of your media network. A media network is a comprehensive list of all the media contacts that are within the scope of your media needs. For example, if you are the manager of a local little league team, your media network will include local and regional media, and possibly state-wide media. On the other hand, if you are a professional athlete that competes both nationally and internationally, then your media network will be much broader, encompassing local, state, national, and international media. The Media Network Sheet in Appendix L will help you gather the information necessary to compile an exhaustive list of contacts. Once you do this, your media network will the hub for most of the publicity that you, your team, or your event receives.

Begin by defining the scope of your network. Decide whether you will need local, regional, state-wide, national, or international contacts. Next, compile a list containing the following information: media source's name (for example, *Los Angeles Times*); contact person (for example, sports editor); source's address; and the contact person's phone and fax numbers. Depending on the scope of your media network, your list can range from five to five- hundred contacts.

MAKING YOUR INITIAL
CONTACT WITH THE MEDIA

Once you have established your media network, you will want to make contact with each media source to let him or her know who you are, a little bit about your program, and how he or she can contact you in the future. You can either make this a really informal initial contact, providing only a limited amount of information, or you can have a formal first contact, supplying all essential statistics and other data.

CREATING INFORMATION
USEFUL TO THE MEDIA

When interacting with the media it is important to do so in a manner that is efficient and succinct. The media representative who receives your material will appreciate both thoroughness and brevity. Since thoroughness and brevity seem to be diametrically opposed, it is your duty to come up with creative approaches to this media dilemma. Four very useful approaches to communicating with the media are: (1) media packets (or press kits); (2) press releases; (3) newsletters; and (4) press conferences. Most of the time you can create your own public relations materials, but if you are a top athlete or the manager of a national team, you may want to consider hiring a professional sports marketer to do this work for you. The key is to catch the media's eye and to intrigue them with your story.

Media Packets

Many professional athletes, team managers, event coordinators, and event sponsors have media packets prepared especially for the purpose of providing the media with comprehensive, useful information. If a media person is interested in learning more about an athlete or event, he or she can merely ask for a media packet rather than a time-consuming interview. If done correctly, a media packet will provide the media representative with all the background information he or she needs to write a story. Additionally, a media person who has read a media packet prior to an interview has the ability to come to an interview armed with intelligent, meaningful questions.

A media packet typically includes a short biographical history on the athlete or team. The biographical portion should clearly state the athlete's or team's name at the top of the page, identify where he or she is living, and how old he or she is currently (or a date of birth). As well, a short description of the athlete's sport and a statement regarding the number of years he or she has been competing should be included in the biographical portion. Other topics that may be discussed in the biographical section are: familial status, other sports that the athlete competes in, the athelete's extracurricular activities, and community/charitable services.

The media packet should also include the athlete's (or team's) competition resume and photographs, both still and action. The resume created in chapter 2 is sufficient for the media packet. And, any photos which you used in your proposal will be fine. As with the proposal, you want to use photographs that highlight who you are and your personality. If you have a unique talent that can be captured on film (that is relevant to the sport), this would be a great place to show it off. You may also want to put a copy of your competition schedule in the media packet so that interested media representatives will know where to contact you at a competition. Lastly, be sure to put your home or office contact information somewhere in the media packet so that they can reach you with ease.

Most media packet materials are placed in a folder to give them a professional appearance. This is not necessary, however, if you cannot afford the expense. Once you create a media packet, be sure that you send it out right away before the materials become outdated. Keep in mind, however, that media kits only need to be prepared once during the season, usually at the beginning. The other methods of contacting the media, newsletters and press releases, can act as a supplement to the media packet.

PRESS RELEASES

Press releases are an efficient and affordable way to keep the media current. A press release is a document prepared with the sole purpose of providing newsworthy information to the media. Press releases are used by most businesses and individuals that want to relay information to the media.

The press release is not as informative and wordy as the newsletter (described below), and it conforms to a standard format. Appendix M provides both a sample press release and a press release worksheet. The author of the press release needs to present information in a way that attracts the media's attention and excites them enough to write about it or contact the author for more information.

Most press releases have some sort of headline or caption at the top of the page to catch the attention of the reader. The headline should be centered on the page, in all capital letters, and bold-faced. The headline should directly relate to the topic of your press release and it should immediately grab the reader's attention and encourage him or her to read the release.

The press release should be double-spaced on 81/2 x 11 white paper. Use only one side of the paper. Press releases can be mailed, faxed, or sent by electronic mail. The release must name a contact person in the organization. This should include the person's full name, title, and phone number. Providing contact information is essential; since your goal is get press coverage, journalists may need to talk to you further and ask follow-up questions.

When writing the text of the press release, begin with the most important information. Then, proceed in order of importance until the end. The essential facts and story must appear in the first paragraph. Always use short and simple sentences to facilitate the reader's rapid comprehension of the document.

Direct press releases to the media person that you identified as the contact on your media network sheet. Within a week of sending the release- or even sooner if it is a very timely story- Follow up to confirm receipt of the press release. As stated above, editors are busy people and are not able to make personal contact with everyone who contacts them. Be patient, if you have a newsworthy story, they will eventually contact you.

Newsletters

Newsletters are a great way to communicate with both sponsors and the media. Many computer programs make drafting newsletters easy and fun. A newsletter is basically an update on the events that have taken place within a specific time frame. During the competition season, a monthly newsletter to sponsors and/or media would be appropriate. Keep in mind, however, that newsletters typically contain more than newsworthy information. So, it may not be a good idea to send your newsletters to media people with whom you do not have a personal relationship. Remember that media editors get a lot of information sent to them, only send newsworthy information! If your newsletters contain this sort of information, go ahead and send them to your media network. Appendix H has a sample newsletter and a newsletter worksheet.

Press Conferences

When circumstances warrant, a press conference can be a very effective way of communicating with the media. A press conference can be used when it is important that new information about an athlete, team, or event be disseminated quickly with an opportunity for comment. One example of an appropriate situation would be the announcement that a nationally acclaimed athlete has made the decision to retire or sign a major deal with a new sponsor. If it is common knowledge that the media is interested in knowing every move of the particular athlete, then it is a safe bet that the media will show up for the announcement. But how do you decide where to hold a press conference for a national athlete when you know that a variety of media sources (i.e. local, state, and national) will be anxious to attend? One option is to conduct a press conference at a national event which all the national media will be attending anyway. This makes the press conference easy to attend, a key factor in setting up these conferences.

Invitations and notices should be sent to media people as much in advance as possible. Usually one week in advance is best but if you have less time to work with, that's ok too. Invitations can be sent by mail, faxed, e-mailed, or personally delivered. Attendance will be low if you rely on word of mouth. It is also polite and proper to personally invite the individuals whom you would like to attend.

Preparation of the press conference should be taken seriously. As stated elsewhere in this book, first impressions last. A room large enough to accommodate all the people attending should be found. The site should be accessible and easy to find. An attentive planner will provide informative materials and refreshments to the media people who attend. Also, when planning a press conference pay particular attention to the format in which you present the content of your information. For example, decide whether you should present the information in a monologue format and reserve questions for the end, or if you should present a slide show. The content of what you have to relay to the media will help determine your delivery.

Before planning a press conference, make certain there is not a better way to communicate the information to the media. In some instances, the information will be better received by the media if it arrives via a press release rather than by attendance at a press conference. Conferences are time- consuming, so do not waste anyone's time.

Building and Keeping Media Relationships

Building relationships with media people takes time. Do not force a relationship, be patient. Be genuine, do not schmooze, because they will be able to identify a schmoozer and will be immediately turned off.

Say "hi!" when you see media people at competitions and events. Be friendly, introduce yourself, and strike up a meaningful conversation. Do not only contact them when you want something. As with any relationship, find common ground and build upon that.

Make contact with your media network before the season begins. Let them know what you are up to, and tell them about who your new sponsors are. Sometimes magazines do pre-season team line-ups and athlete biographies, so you will want to get your new statistics to them early in the year.

Another way to keep contact with media people is with holiday and birthday cards. Only pursue this line of contact if you have an established relationship with the media person. This gesture will show your sincerity and help them remember you.

Straight from the Media's Mouth to Your Ears

"Don't blow off appointments. As a member of the media, I have a lot to cover in a weekend of racing. Regardless of your status in the industry, I will always feel better about someone who can keep their appointments. If I get blown off more than once, without a legitimate excuse ("I had to go for a spin to loosen up my legs" doesn't cut it), I'll find someone else to inter-

view, and they'll get the exposure, and the first shot at the inter-view next time.

"I need people who not only make news, but who make my job easier, and if I have to choose between one or the other, I'll always choose the more helpful riders.

"Granted, in all situations, there are members of the press who do not respect a rider's privacy or needs, and that is a different issue, but if you make a conscious effort to be courteous to the press, and keep your appointments, you'll get a lot further than many of today's top riders who give the impression that they just don't have time for the media."

— MATT LANNING, PUBLIC RELATIONS/MEDIA COORDINATOR

"Do make yourself available to the media. Be open, patient, honest, and courteous. It is very helpful when athletes send us press releases, and when athletes give us up-to-date resumes. Also, be sure to treat all members of the media (print and TV) with equal respect."

— LIZA AND RICHARD MUHL, SPORTS JOURNAL

"When sending press releases and story ideas to the media, be sure that you have researched the market of each particular media source. You should only send materials to those media outlets that will have an interest in what you have to say. And, only send newsworthy information."

— MARTI STEPHEN, MOUNTAIN BIKE EDITOR, VELONEWS

"Don't assume that editors have a lot of time to chat on the telephone. We are really busy and appreciate it when people communicate with us by means other than the telephone. "

— STEPHEN

"Be courteous. As a member of the media, I can be your best friend. My job is to give you exposure, I don't need a lot of attention, but I would like the respect of knowing that you acknowledge my need to get a quick interview, or your thoughts on a race. I may not always know what is the best time for you, so let me know if there is a better time for you, then keep your word to meet with me. When you do acknowledge, eye contact is always a good sign that you appreciate my effort to interview you. Even if you've just finished a race, and are wiped out, a quick acknowledgment that we're in a conversation is greatly appreciated."

— LANNING

Fan and Crowd Appreciation

One of the easiest and most fun ways to obtain good publicity is to make yourself available to your fans and the crowds at events. As an athlete, you should take the time to sign autographs when asked. You should also make yourself available to fans at competition venues. If you have fans, assume they want to talk to you. When you take the time to chat with them you create a positive persona for yourself. People like to know they can relate to you, and have a moment of your time.

As a team manager, you should have posters made of the top athletes on your team for autograph sessions at events. The benefits of doing this are three-fold: (1) you attract spectators to your booth and give them an opportunity to see your products; (2) you send them home with a poster which serves as constant reminder of the team's sponsors; and (3) you generate good will.

As an event coordinator, you have the job of generating

Margo Carroll, M2 Images

**PODIUM FINISHERS SHOULD HANG OUT AFTER EVENTS TO BE
INTERVIEWED BY MEDIA PEOPLE.**

crowds. One way to do this is to appreciate the crowds when
they are at the event. You can have raffles, giveaways, and
autograph sessions with the pros. Also, be sure that you create an event that is exciting, action-packed, and enjoyable. If
you can avoid charging spectator entry fees, do it. Many
more people are likely to patronize the event if its free.

Athlete sponsorship, team sponsorship, and sports event
marketing are complicated, but exciting. The key to success

is two-fold: (1) you must behave in a professional manner, and (2) you must value your own talent or the team's, or the worth of the event, in a realistic manner. In most circumstances, qualified athletes, teams, or events will obtain some level of sponsorship from some company. When you find a sponsor, be sure to be an honest and forthright person, appreciate your fans, and most of all have fun. With all the work you have done, you deserve it!

CHERI ELLIOTT TAKES TIME OUT OF HER COMPETITION WEEKEND TO POSE FOR A PHOTO WITH SOME OF HER FANS.

INDIVIDUAL ATHLETE PROPOSAL BUDGET

Athlete name: _____ Year: _____

Expense Category	*Cost*	*Total*
Resume paper		
Presentation folders (optional)		
Envelopes		
Printing costs		
Photo reproduction (optional)		
Color copy		
Black and white copy		
Photo duplication		
Video reproduction (optional)		
Postage		
TOTAL PER PROPOSAL	$	$

How many proposals will you be sending out to companies?

_____

Calculate your total costs:

$_____(cost per proposal) X ___ number of proposals = _____

Can you afford this expense? YES NO

If your answer is NO, where can you cut corners to save money?

1. Send fewer proposals, if possible.
2. Do not use presentation folders (this will save you postage, too).
3. Send fewer color-copied photos.
4. Only send videos upon request. Mention video availability.

INDIVIDUAL ATHLETE SINGLE EVENT BUDGET

Event name: _____

Event location: _____

Event dates: _____

Expense Category	Minimum Needed	Ideal Amount
Entry fees		
Travel Airfare/Bus Car rental Gasoline Highway tolls Hotel accommodations Food		
Competition equipment		
Training equipment		
Competition clothing		
Massage/Chiropractic		
Trainer/Fitness consultant		
Gym fees		
Nutritional supplements		
Misc. publicity expenses		
Other event expenses		
Other travel expenses		
TOTAL		

INDIVIDUAL ATHLETE OVERALL BUDGET

Athlete name: _____ Year: _____

Expense Category	Minimum Needed	Ideal Amount
Entry fees		

Travel
  Airfare/Bus
  Car rental
  Gasoline
  Highway tolls
  Hotel accommodations
  Food		

Competition equipment		
Training equipment		
Competition clothing		
Massage/Chiropractic		
Trainer/Fitness consultant		
Gym fees		
Nutritional supplements		
Misc. publicity expenses		
Other event expenses		
Other travel expenses		
TOTAL		

RESUME WORKSHEET

Name: _____

Nickname: _____

Address: _____

_____

Phone: (Home) _____(Work) _____

Fax: E-mail address: _____

Birthdate: _____

Sport(s): _____

Level/Category: No. of years in the sport(s): _____

Current Year's Results (Year 1):

COMPETITION DATE	COMPETITION NAME	VENUE NAME	YOUR PLACING	TITLES/AWARDS GIVEN

SEASON'S TITLES/AWARDS/OTHER RECOGNITION: _____

_____

Last Year's Results (Year 2):

COMPETITION DATE	COMPETITION NAME	VENUE NAME	YOUR PLACING	TITLES/AWARDS GIVEN

Season's titles/awards/other recognition: _____

_____

Participation in activities related to the sport (non-competition):

_____

_____

Previous/Current Sponsors: _____

_____

Educational History:

High school degree: _____

College degree: _____

Post graduate degree: _____

Certificate program: _____

References:

1. Name _____

    Association _____

    Telephone number (   ) _____FAX (   ) _____

2. Name _____

    Association _____

    Telephone number (   ) _____FAX (   )_____

3. Name _____

    Association _____

    Telephone number (   ) _____FAX (   )_____

Hobbies: _____

_____

SAMPLE RESUMES AND HEADINGS

Sample Resumes: One page

Jane Doe

Professional Snowboarder
123 Nowhere Lane
Nowhereville, CA 91234
Home (123) 456-7890 Work (123) 555-5555

1996 Rookie of the Year

1998 Goals and Objectives
Goals for 1998 include placing consistently in the top five at all national events.

1997 Season Results   Event Location   Giant Slalom
(your data)

1996 Season Results   Event Location   Giant Slalom
Elite Category Rookie of the Year

Special Additions
(your data)
Recommendations available upon request.

Resume of professional cyclist Cheri Elliott as of 8/5/97

CHERI ELLIOTT

1997 NORBA National Downhill Champion
1997 ESPN Winter Extreme Games Dual Speed Gold Medalist
1996 US Mountain Challenge Series National #1 Dual Slalom Champion
1996 NORBA National #2 Dual Slalom Champion
1995 ESPN Summer Extreme Games Downhill Gold Medalist
1994 NORBA National #1 Dual Slalom Champion
Only Female "BMX Hall of Fame" Inductee
Four Time World and National BMX Champion
Professional Mountain Bike Racer / Downhill and Dual Slalom Specialist
3941 Park Drive, 20-210 El Dorado Hills, CA 95762

1997 SEASON   *1997 Winter Extreme Games Gold Medalist*

Event	Dual Slalom	Downhill
Extreme Games: Big Bear, CA		1st
Cactus Cup: Scottsdale, AZ	1st	
NORBA #1: Big Bear, CA	3rd	2nd
World Cup #2: Nevegal, Italy	1st	
NORBA #2: Seven Springs, Penn.	5th	7th
NORBA #3: Mt. Snow, Vermont	5th	8th
World Cup #4: Mont-Ste-Anna, Qbec	3rd	4th
NORBA #4: Mammoth, CA	2nd	2nd
NORBA #5: Seattle, WA	2nd	5th

1996 SEASON   *1996 USMCS National #1 Dual Slalom Champion*
1996 NORBA National #2 Dual Slalom Champion
1996 NORBA National #10 Downhill Champion

Event	Dual Slalom	Downhill
Cactus Cup: Phoenix, AZ	2nd	
Sea Otter Classic: Montery, CA	3rd	
World Cup #1: Panticosa, Spain	1st	
World Cup #2: Nevegal, Italy	1st	10th
NCS #1: Mt. Snow, VT	2nd	
NCS #2: Traverse City, MI		8th
NCS #3: Big Bear, CA	2nd	8th
NCS #4: Deer Valley, UT	3rd	8th
NCS # 5: Mammoth Lakes, CA	1st	7th
DH Mania (USMCS): Deer Valley, UT	2nd	5th
DH Mania (USMCS): North Star, CA	1st	5th

CHERI ELLIOTT   *page 2*

1995 SEASON   *1995 Extreme Games World Downhill Champion*
                   1995 NORBA National #7 Downhill Champion
                   1995 NORBA National #3 Dual Slalom Champion

1994 SEASON   *NORBA National #1 Dual Slalom Champion*
(1st Year)   *NORBA National #13 Downhill Champion*

SPECIAL   • Stylish jumping exclusively captured in an original
                     watercolor painting by John D. Wibberly, now distrib-
                     uted on a postcard.
                   • Only woman to ever qualify in the top 10 men's dual
                     slalom. Vail, CO 1994 World Championships.
                   • Co-authored *"The Athlete's Guide to Sponsorship."*

BICYCLING   **Bicycle Motocross (BMX) /** 1980 - 1985
ROOTS   • Only woman to ever be inducted into the BMX Hall of
                     Fame. (1989)
                   • Nominated the Greatest Female BMXer of All Time.
                     (1993)
                   • Only BMX racer to ever receive four consecutive World
                     and National Titles.
                   • Only female to compete nationally against the guys and
                     win.
                   • Known as a "living legend" for achieving countless titles,
                     beating the guys, and for big air, radical jumping.

EDUCATION   **B.S. Business Administration**
                   Concentrated in Real Estate and Land Use.
                   • Dean's Honor List, every semester.
                   • Received Scholarship: Academic/Athletic
                   • Played Intercollegiate Varsity Basketball / Division 1

Sample Resume Headings

Sample Heading 1

Jane Doe
123 Nowhere Lane
Nowhereville, CA 91234
Home (123) 456-7890 Work (123) 555-5555

Sample Heading 2

JANE DOE

123 Nowhere Lane
Nowhereville, CA 91234
(123) 456-7890

Sample Heading 3

Jane Doe

123 Nowhere Lane   Home: (123) 456-7890
Nowhereville, CA 91234   Work: (123) 555-5555

Sample Heading 4

Jane Doe
123 Nowhere Lane
Nowhereville, CA 91234
(123) 456-7890

SAMPLE COVER LETTER

Date

Contact Name
Company Name
Company Address
Company Address

Dear Mr./Ms. Contact Person:

Having been the National Champion in the expert class of cross-country mountain biking for the past two years, I will be entering the professional ranks next season. I am interested in endorsing your ABC line of shifters and derailleurs.

My first experience with mountain bike racing was in 1991 when I entered a race that was put on by the local college. I immediately formed an attachment to the sport and decided that I was good enough for competition. Since that time I have competed in over 50 cross-country races and have won 26 of them. My dominance in the expert class has encouraged me to make the move into the pro's.

ABC's commitment to mountain bike racing is impressive. I am interested in continuing the long line of successful athletes who have given terrific exposure opportunities to ABC in return for sponsorship. Specifically, I would like to receive product for three bikes, for both training and competition, and performance bonuses. In return, ABC would have the right to use my name and likeness in its advertising campaign. Additionally, I am an experienced mechanic and would be willing to act as team mechanic at all of the national events.

I have enclosed my resume and photos. I look forward to speaking with you soon.

Sincerely,

(Your Signature)

Your Name

SAMPLE FOLLOW-UP AND THANK YOU LETTERS

SAMPLE FOLLOW-UP LETTER

Date

Contact Name
Company Name
Company Address
Company Address

Mr./Ms. Contact Person:

Three weeks ago I sent you a proposal for sponsorship. I am still very interested in using (insert product name) during competition and endorsing (insert company name).

To refresh your memory, I am a cross-country mountain bike racer and currently hold the 1996 Expert Class Championship title. I will be racing in the pro class next season.

I look forward to your response and to discussing opportunities for sponsorship soon.

Sincerely,

(Your Signature)

Your Name

NOTE: The rules regarding spelling and grammar apply to all subsequent correspondence. Remember to be as professional as possible.

Sample Thank You Letters

Rejection Response

Date

Contact Name
Company Name
Company Address
Company Address

Dear Mr./Ms. Contact Name:

Thank you for considering my proposal for sponsorship. Please keep my information on file in case your needs change in the future. Otherwise, I look forward to resubmitting a proposal next year. I wish you and your athletes a successful season.

Sincerely,

(Your Signature)

Your Name

Acceptance Response

Date

Contact Name
Company Name
Company Address
Company Address

Dear Mr./Ms. Contact Name:

Thank you for making me a (insert Company Name) sponsored athlete. I look forward to working with you and the other athletes in an effort to successfully promote your company's product(s). Please let me know if I can assist you in any way in preparing for the upcoming season.
Thanks again.

Sincerely,

(Your Signature)

Your Name

COMPETITION-VENUE SCHEDULE WORKSHEET

_____Competition-Venue Schedule
(Year #)

EVENT DATE	EVENT TITLE	EVENT LOCATION

PROPOSAL RECORD SHEET

Company Name	Date Sent	Follow-Up #1	Follow-Up #2	Company Response	Official Sponsor?	Thank you Sent

NEWSLETTER WORKSHEET
AND SAMPLE NEWSLETTER

NEWSLETTER WORKSHEET

Dates covered in this newsletter: _____

Announcements (For example: new sponsors, addition of
team members, web site developments, etc.): _____

_____

_____

_____

Competition results within newsletter's time frame (event
name, location, placing): _____

_____

_____

_____

Awards and other recognition received within newsletter's
time frame: _____

_____

Media coverage received within newsletter's time frame (state
media source, date, and type of coverage): _____

_____

Upcoming important dates (events, seminars, trade shows,
you will attend): _____

_____

Requests for product or other promotional items (shirts,
patches, stickers): _____

_____

Other relevant information: _____

_____

SAMPLE NEWSLETTER

CHERI ELLIOTT NEWS

A JED Sports Management Publication
3941 Park Drive, Suite 20-210
El Dorado Hills, CA 95762

Volume III Issue I

January 1998

CONGRATULATIONS Cheri! The National Champ Attains Two Silver Medals at the Winter X-Games Making her the OVERALL TOP Mountain Bike Finisher for the Week!

Cheri continues her dominant podium ways by taking second place in both the Dual Downhill and Dual Speed event at the Winter Extreme Games. She just missed two golds by a hair. She proudly says, "It was awesome! I improved so much on the snow this year as opposed to last year. In the Dual Downhill last year I didn't even qualify I was so awful. Last week was a great triumph and a great way to start the year!"

Not only was Cheri the **OVERALL TOP MOUNTAIN BIKE FINISHER** for the week, she also stood out among the others by getting BIG AIR over the thirty foot triples, with style and grace in the Dual Downhill event. And, in the Speed Event, Cheri and Elka Brustart broke the 70mph mark. Cheri was clocked at 70.3mph -- faster than most of the men. Cheri boasted, "We ladies put on a great show. In the Speed Event, there is almost no gap between men and women. Elka and I could have competed against the men and given them a run for their money! We had lots of fun."

Attention 1998 Sponsors! Cheri's Special X-Games Uniform Was Ripped to Shreds!

Due to the many spikes in her tires, combined with a gnarly crash Cheri had on the first day of practice, her special X-Games uniform with proper logos ripped to shreds. She had to run some random moto gear in the Dual Downhill, and Phil Tinsman's rubber suit in the Speed event (looked just like Cheri's special outfit, but not with all the proper logos). In the speed event, any sponsor stickers Cheri had, she put them on her faring. Cheri grunted, "I just didn't think I would need more than ONE suit for ONE race. Next year we'll make two!" Cheri's official 1998 National Champion uniform, with proper logos, is still in production.

Attention 1998 Sponsors! Welcome Aboard!

Cheri Elliott wants to thank all her official 1998 sponsors. She looks forward to a successful 1998, and beyond. She wants to promote her sponsors properly, so please send hats, t-shirts, stickers, & patches ect.... T-shirts -- L and XL.

3941 Park Dr
Suite 20-
El Dorado Hills, CA 95

BUDGET WORKSHEET - TEAM

TEAM BUDGET

Team name: _____ Year: _____

No. of team members: _____

No. of venues team will attend: _____

Expense Category	Minimum Needed	Ideal Amount
Entry fees		

Travel
  Airfare/Bus
  Car rental
  Gasoline
  Highway tolls
  Lodging
  Food		

Athlete salaries		
Athlete performance incentives		
Marketing campaign		

Administrative costs
  Team Manager
  Massage therapist
  Mechanic, etc.		

Trainer/Fitness consultant		
Team vehicle(s)		
Expo tents/Display casses		

Nutritional supplements		
Miscellaneous		
Other event expenses		
Other travel expenses		
TOTAL		

SAMPLE BUSINESS MANAGEMENT AGREEMENT

This Business Management Agreement is entered into this (date here) by and between <u>ABC Sports Agency</u>, herein referred to as "Manager," and <u>(Athlete's name)</u>, herein referred to as "Athlete." This contract shall terminate on (date here) or at such time when either party shall serve the other party with 60 (sixty) days written notice. Any contracts which Manager has negotiated for Athlete that have not lapsed at the close of the termination period shall remain CURRENT AND PAYABLE as agreed between Manager and Athlete.

IN CONSIDERATION OF THEIR MUTUAL PROMISES AND AGREEMENTS HEREIN CONTAINED, THE PARTIES HEREBY AGREE AS FOLLOWS:

I. SCOPE OF AGREEMENT

1. The purpose of this Agreement is to employ the Manager for the express purpose of procurement and negotiating of all terms of all endorsements, and to manage the business affairs of Athlete as described in this agreement.

1.01 The Athlete's decision as to which endorsements shall be accepted shall be conclusive and binding on the Manager.

II. DUTIES OF THE MANAGER

2.01 Management under this contract includes, <u>but is not limited to</u>, finding endorsements for Athlete and negotiating terms of contracts; procuring corporate and other endorsements for

Athlete and negotiating all terms of those contracts; obtaining press coverage for Athlete; managing daily affairs between Athlete and his or her sponsors; preparing and sending required race information to sponsors concerning Athlete's competition results and amounts due; collecting payment from sponsors; receiving products sent to Athlete from respective sponsors and forwarding them to Athlete. Additional services may be agreed upon in writing by both parties.

2.02 Manager agrees to use his or her best efforts to provide prompt, courteous, efficient and professional services to promote the work of the Athlete.

2.03 Manager shall, at the request of Athlete, be prepared at all times to represent Athlete at a press conference or other official or unofficial event.

2.04 Manager shall refrain from engaging in unlawful conduct or conduct involving fraud, deceit, or misrepresentation.

III. COMPENSATION

3.01 In consideration for the Manager's efforts, the Athlete agrees to pay the Manager 10% (ten percent) of the compensation received by Athlete during the term of this contract plus expenses. (See, Provision 3.03 below regarding "expenses.")

3.02 Athlete agrees to pay Manager an initial contract $50, signing fee for each endorsement sponsor obtained on behalf of Athlete.

3.03 Athlete agrees to pay reasonable additional <u>expenses</u> that Manager may incur in representing Athlete on site (at races, press conferences, etc.). This includes, but is not limited to, airfare, hotel expenses, car rental, meals. Manager shall notify Athlete prior to the use of additional expenses. All additional expenses shall be approved by Athlete.

3.04 Athlete agrees to pay reasonable additional <u>expenses</u> that Manager may incur when drafting sponsorship proposals, negotiating sponsorship deals, preparing media packets, and other related tasks. Manager agrees to not exceed the annually budgeted amount of $_____ unless he/she receives prior approval from Athlete.

3.05 Manager shall continue to receive 10% (ten percent) of any and all compensation Athlete earns as the result of a contract negotiated by Manager that has not lapsed at the termination of this contract.

3.06 Athlete shall be billed the first of each month. Athlete agrees to pay the Manager within 30 (thirty) days of issuance of billing statement.

IV. Duties of the Athlete

4.01 Athlete agrees to provide Manager with current and accurate information regarding Athlete's abilities and performance.

4.02 Athlete shall at all times adhere to the terms of this contract, the terms of <u>all</u> contracts that Manager and Athlete negotiate with third parties, and act in a way which will not damage

Athlete's reputation, the reputation of Manager, or the reputation of any third parties with whom Athlete and Manager are associated.

V. Amending the Agreement

5.01 Both Manger and Athlete agree that this contract may be amended with the written consent of both parties. No terms that are not herein outlined or in the "Fee Agreement" shall be binding unless there is an express amendment drawn up by Manager and signed by both the Manager and the Athlete.

VI. Termination of the Agreement

6.01 This Agreement shall terminate at such time when either party shall serve on the other party 60 (sixty) days written notice.

6.02 Any and all contracts which Manager has negotiated for the Athlete which have not lapsed at the close of the termination period shall remain CURRENT AND PAYABLE pursuant to Provision 3.04 of this Agreement.

VII.General and Administrative Provisions

7.01 This Agreement shall be subject to and governed by the laws of [California].

7.02 In the event of breach of this Agreement by the Athlete, the Manager may recover from the Athlete any and all damages that the Manager may sustain as a result of the breach of this Agreement. This includes the Manager's legal fees.

7.03 In the event of breach of this Agreement by the Manager, Athlete may recover from Manager any or all damages that the Athlete my sustain as a result of the breach of this Agreement.

7.04 Athlete and Manager agree that all disputes will be referred to arbitration with in thirty (30) days of the agrieved party notifying the other party of the dispute. Arbitrator will be chosen from the list of AAA arbitrators.

This agreement is entered into in a spirit of friendship and cooperation. Both parties mutually agree to assist the other in making this a pleasant relationship.

Date   Athlete Agent

Date   Athlete, Athlete's Sport

DISCLAIMER This is only a sample agreement. Any agreements should be reviewed by a qualified athlete agent or attorney.

SAMPLE SPONSORSHIP AGREEMENT

This Sponsorship Agreement is entered into on this January 1, 1999 by and between (Company X), herein referred to as "COMPANY" and (ATHLETE's full name), herein referred to as "ATHLETE."

1. Term: This Sponsorship Agreement shall commence on January 1, 1999 and shall terminate on December 31, 1999. This agreement covers a period of one (1) season.

2. Exclusivity: No competitive company will be granted sponsorship rights during the term of the contract. ATHLETE will exclusively use COMPANY products in all sports-related and media activities.

3. Advertising/Grant of Endorsement: ATHLETE agrees to allow his/her name and likeness to be used in COMPANY advertising programs in connection with product line. COMPANY's right to use name and likeness shall expire six (6) months after the termination of this Sponsorship Agreement. Photo shoots and special appearances will require advance notice for the ATHLETE as to time and location. All expenses will be the responsibility of the COMPANY.

4. Confidentiality: COMPANY and ATHLETE agree that all terms of this agreement are confidential, and agree not to disclose any of the terms contained in this agreement, including those terms relating to compensation.

5. Product Allotment: COMPANY will supply ATHLETE with an initial ten (10) widgets before the season starts. If and when more widgets are needed, it is the ATHLETE's responsibility to request them. A maximum of twenty (20) widgets will be allowed for the entire 1999 season.

6. Signing Bonus: A signing bonus of $5000 is payable to ATH-LETE by COMPANY in three installments, $1500 on January 15, $1500 on March 15, and $2000 on July 15.

7. Victory Bonuses: It is the ATHLETE's responsibility to request a victory incentive payment, in writing via FAX or US mail, with a copy of the official event results. Payments are due thirty (30) days after receipt of official results. A bonus cap of $10,000 will be enforced by COMPANY.*

* Bonuses for National events only.

1st Place	$ 500
2nd Place	$ 300
3rd Place	$ 150

This agreement is entered into in a spirit of friendship and cooperation. Both parties nutually agree to assist the other in making this a pleasant relationship.

Athlete's full name   Date

Company's Representative   Date

MEDIA NETWORK WORKSHEET

LOCAL AND REGIONAL MEDIA CONTACTS

(1) Media name: _____ Type: _____

Media contact: _____ Title: _____

Address: _____

_____

Phone No. ( ) _____ Fax No. ( ) _____

Responses: _____

_____

(2) Media name: _____ Type: _____

Media contact: _____ Title: _____

Address: _____

_____

Phone No. ( ) _____ Fax No. ( ) _____

Responses: _____

_____

(3) Media name: _____ Type: _____

Media contact: _____ Title: _____

Address: _____

_____

Phone No. ( ) _____ Fax No. ( ) _____

Responses: _____

_____

(4) Media name: _____ Type: _____

Media contact: _____ Title: _____

Address: _____

_____

Phone No. ( ) _____ Fax No. ( ) _____

Responses: _____

_____

STATEWIDE MEDIA CONTACTS

(1) Media name: _____ Type: _____

Media contact: _____ Title: _____

Address: _____

_____

Phone No. ( ) _____ Fax No. ( ) _____

Responses: _____

_____

(2) Media name: _____ Type: _____

Media contact: _____ Title: _____

Address: _____

_____

Phone No. ( ) _____ Fax No. ( ) _____

Responses: _____

_____

(3) Media name: _____ Type: _____

Media contact: _____ Title: _____

Address: _____

_____

Phone No. ( ) _____ Fax No. ( ) _____

Responses: _____

_____

(4) Media name: _____ Type: _____

Media contact: _____ Title: _____

Address: _____

_____

Phone No. ( ) _____ Fax No. ( ) _____

Responses: _____

_____

NATIONAL MEDIA CONTACTS

(1) Media name: _____Type: _____

Media contact: _____Title: _____

Address: _____

_____

Phone No. (   ) _____Fax No. (   ) _____

Responses: _____

_____

(2) Media name: _____Type: _____

Media contact: _____Title: _____

Address: _____

_____

Phone No. (   ) _____Fax No. (   ) _____

Responses: _____

_____

(3) Media name: _____Type: _____

Media contact: _____Title: _____

Address: _____

_____

Phone No. (   ) _____Fax No. (   ) _____

Responses: _____

_____

(4) Media name: _____Type: _____

Media contact: _____Title: _____

Address: _____

_____

Phone No. (   ) _____Fax No. (   ) _____

Responses: _____

_____

INTERNATIONAL MEDIA CONTACTS

(1) Media name: _____Type: _____

Media contact: _____Title: _____

Address: _____

_____

Phone No. (   ) _____Fax No. (   ) _____

Responses: _____

_____

Language(s) spoken: _____

(2) Media name: _____Type: _____

Media contact: _____Title: _____

Address: _____

_____

Phone No. (   ) _____Fax No. (   ) _____

Responses: _____

_____

Language(s) spoken: _____

PRESS RELEASE WORKSHEET

FOR IMMEDIATE RELEASE, _____
                                             (date)

Media contact: _____ — _____
                    (Name)   (Phone no.)

**CAPTION IN BOLD CAPITAL LETTERS SUMMARIZING
THE CONTENT OF YOUR PRESS RELEASE AND AIMED
TO CATCH THE ATTENTION OF THE READER!**

_____

_____

_____

Paragraph one — Who and What?

Paragraph two — When and Where?

Paragraph three — What's Next and When?

SAMPLE PRESS RELEASE

<u>FOR IMMEDIATE RELEASE</u> — ,
Media Contact Jennifer Drury, JED Sports Management (916) 555-5555

LEADING NATIONAL DOWNHILL MOUNTAIN BIKE RACER IS NORTHERN CALIFORNIA'S CHERI ELLIOTT

Cameron Park, CA— When talking about champions consistency prevails over sheer dominance. Cheri Elliott, Sacramento born and raised, is living proof. On August 2, 1997, Cheri Elliott took her third straight second place downhill victory of the season in the NORBA National Championship Series. Cheri's consistency put her in FIRST PLACE in the overall championship series with one race left.

All of Cheri's off-season training paid off yesterday when she stood atop the winner's podium and was handed the leader's jersey. With one race left, the national finals in Utah (August 22 and 23), it looks like Northern California may be home to the nation's best downhill mountain bike racer —- Cheri Elliott.

To put things in perspective, the top four women in the nation are given the honor to compete on behalf of the United States at the world championships in September. Cheri is definitely going for the U.S.A. The world Championships are held in Switzerland this year the third week of September.

We are all proud of Cheri here at JED Sports Management and want to share her successes with her community, as we know people will be both interested and proud.

##

Sponsorship Stories or Tips
to Share with Other Athletes

Please share your favorite sponsorship story or tip with other athletes! If you have a story that you feel belongs in the next edition of The Athlete"s Guide to Sponsorship, please send it to us, at:

JED Sports Management
c/o Jennifer Drury
3941 Park Drive, Suite 20-210
El Dorado Hills, CA 95762
JEDSPORTS@MINDSYNC.COM

We will make sure that you receive credit for your contribution if your story or tip appears in the next edition.

Be sure to include your name, address, telephone number, and where you are from so you will receive proper credit for your contribution.

You may also write the above address with feedback about the book or suggestions you have for future editions. Let us know if you were successful in your endeavors!

Other books from VeloPress

Perfect Circles *by Greg Moody*
Team Haven rides again! The long-anticipated sequel to *Two Wheels* begins with the mysterious death of a professional cyclist in Belgium, and takes the Haven peloton through the grueling Tour de France. Will Ross is back in great form as the aging team lieutenant determined to place his team in le Tour, cycling's most prestigious international event. • 400 pp • Paperback.
1-884737-44-7 • P-CIR $12.95

The Cyclist's Training Bible *by Joe Friel*
Hailed as a major breakthrough in training for competitive cycling, this book helps take cyclists from where they are to where they want to be — the podium. • 288 pp. • Photos, charts, diagrams • Paperback.
1-884737-21-8 • P-BIB $19.95

Off-Season Training for Cyclists *by Edmund R. Burke, Ph.D.*
Burke takes you through everything you need to know about winter training—indoor workouts, weight training, cross-training, periodization and more. 168 pp. • photos • Paperback.
1-994737-40-4 • P-OFF $14.95

Zinn & the Art of Mountain Bike Maintenance, 2nd Edition *by Lennard Zinn*
Guides you through every aspect of mountain-bike maintenance, repair and troubleshooting in a succinct, idiot-proof format. • 288 pp • Illustrations • Paperback
1-884737-47-1 • P-ZIN $17.95

Bicycle Racing in the Modern Era *from the editors of* VeloNews
These 63 articles represent the best in cycling journalism over the past quarter century. • 218 pp. • Paperback.
1-884737-32-3 • P-MOD $19.95

Tales from the Toolbox *by Scott Parr with Rupert Guinness*
In his years as a Motorola team mechanic, Scott Parr saw it all. Get the inside dirt on the pro peloton and the guys who really make it happen … the mechanics. • 168 pp. • Paperback.
1-884737-39-0 • P-TFT $14.95

VeloNews **Training Diary** *by Joe Friel*
The world's most popular training diary for cyclists. Allows you to record every facet of training with plenty of room for notes. Non-dated, so you can start any time of the year. • 240 pp. • Spiral-bound.
1-884737-42-0 • P-DIA $12.95

Inside Triathlon **Training Diary** *by Joe Friel*
Combines the best in quantitative and qualitative training notation. Designed to help you attain your best fitness ever. Non-dated, so you can start at any time of the year. • 240 pp. • Spiral-bound.
1-884737-41-2 • P-IDI $12.95

Single-Track Mind *by Paul Skilbeck*
The right combination of scientific training information, bike-handling skills, nutrition, mental training, and a proven year-round training plan. • 128 pp. • Photos, charts, diagrams • Paperback.
1-884737-10-2 • P-STM $19.95

Weight Training for Cyclists *by Eric Schmitz and Ken Doyle*
Written from the premise that optimum cycling performance demands total body strength, this book informs the serious cyclist on how to increase strength with weight training, as cycling alone cannot completely develop the muscle groups used while riding. • 160 pp. • 40 b/w photos • Paperback.
1-884737-43-9 • P-WTC $14.95

Cyclo-cross *by Simon Burney*
A must read for anyone brave enough to ride their road bike downhill through the mud. • 200 pp. • Photos, charts, diagrams • Paperback.
1-884737-20-X • P-CRS $14.95

The Mountain Biker's Cookbook *by Jill Smith*
Healthy and delicious recipes from the world's best mountain-bike racers. The ideal marriage between calories and the perfect way to burn them off. • 152 pp. • Paperback.
1-884737-23-4 • P-EAT $14.95

Barnett's Manual *by John Barnett*
Regarded by professionals world-wide as the final word in bicycle maintenance. • 950 pp. • Illustrations, diagrams, charts • Five-ring loose-leaf binder.
1-884737-16-1 • P-BNT $149.95

Half-Wheel Hell *by Maynard Hershon*
Hershon explores our perception of ourselves and our sport with humor and sensitivity. • 134 pp. • Paperback.
1-884737-05-6 • P-HWH $13.95

Tour de France THE 75TH ANNIVERSARY BICYCLE RACE *by Robin Magowan*
Magowan's fluid prose style brings to life the most contested Tour de France as if it were yesterday. • 208 pp. • Photos and stage profiles • Hardbound.
1-884737-13-7 • P-MAG $24.95

Eddy Merckx *by Rik Vanwalleghem*
Discover the passion and fear that motivated the world's greatest cyclist. The man they called "the cannibal" is captured like never before in this lavish coffee-table book. • 216 pp. • 24 color & 165 B/W photos • Hardback.
1-884737-22-6 • P-EDY $49.95

Bobke *by Bob Roll*
If Hunter S. Thompson and Dennis Rodman had a boy, he would write like Bob Roll: rough-hewn, poetic gonzo. Roll's been there and has the T-shirts to prove it. • 124 pp. • Photos • Paperback.
1-884737-12-9 • P-BOB $16.95

A Season in Turmoil *by Samuel Abt*
Abt traces the differing fortunes of American road racers Lance Armstrong and Greg LeMond through the 1994 season. Revealing, in-depth interviews show the raw exuberance of Armstrong as he becomes the top U.S. road cycling star, while LeMond sinks toward an unwanted retirement. • 178 pp. • B/W photos • Paperback.
1-884737-09-9 • P-SIT $14.95

For ordering or more information, please call VeloPress toll-free: 800/234-8356 or visit our Website: www.velocatalogue.com